A Family

Robert Greenler

A Family

Cover and author photos: John Greenler

With thanks to...

Corry Greenler
who made a book out of a batch of short stories

and Alex Greenler
who helped with layout and getting rid of pesky mistakes.

Contents

Introduction 7

Part One: My Family Growing Up 9
A Letter to the Future 11
First Communication 14
A Day at Horicon Marsh 16
Ring Around the Rosie 18
Something I Almost Didn't Do 20
A Dissatisfied Student 21
The Farmhouse, the Barn, and the Playhouse 24

Part Two: Influence of My Parents 29
Beekeeping 31
My Mother's Speech 35
My Father—Stretching the Limits 36

Part Three: My Growing Up 41
Staying Up Late 43
First Airplane Ride 45
Threshing Day 47
A Small Business in a Small Town 50
A Gift 53
Write it Down! 55
A Trip to Remember 59
My UFO 61
My Song-Writing Career 63
Firefighting 67
The Trip Home 72
A Canoe Trip 76

Senses of Humor..79
Roundup 81
A Walk Around the World 84
Japanese Writing...88
A Satisfying Ovation...90
Monarch Butterflies 92

Part Four: Reflections Later in Life..................95
A Path Not Taken 97
A Life Between 100
There Has to Be A Better Way 102
A Wealthy Man 105
Sycamore Tree...109
Small Towns 112
Bike Riding...114
If I Were 20 Years Younger 118
A Lifetime of Reading...121
It's About Time 125
Thoughts of Winter 129

Introduction

These are stories in *A Family* with similarities to and differences from every other family, but they are about *My Family*. The focus is on my parents, my three children, and six grandchildren. That limited choice is somewhat arbitrary, relying on events stored in my own memory, not historical documents. The omission of many significant others says nothing about their importance to this family story.

The rough organization of the book describes:
1. My family growing up.
2. The influence of my parents.
3. My growing up.
4. Miscellaneous reflections later in life.

The stories in this book describe the basis for a profound feeling that I am among the most fortunate of men.

Part One:

My Family Growing Up

A Letter to the Future

October 2019

> *To my six grandchildren:*
> *Skye and Ellie, Alex and Corry, Scott and Tommy*
> *From: Your Grandbob*

Two months ago, the six of you, currently living on the west coast, the east coast, in Georgia and Canada, organized and pulled off a total-surprise gathering, when all of you and your parents appeared for a two-month-early, 90th year birthday party for me. And the most precious gift you could possibly have given me were letters from each of you, and each of your parents, listing ten memories of times you spent with me. I savored the letters and read only one per day to make the gift last for a couple of weeks.

Those wonderful letters made me think about the two grandfathers I had. My relation with them was not nearly as close as my relation with you. However, I'll tell you about a couple of trivial incidents with each of them.

I remember my Grandpa Mallett as a dour old man. I inherited a personal diary he kept as a young, unmarried man. He quit his job as a tinsmith in Defiance, Ohio and headed out west to see some of the world. A couple of times he stopped along the way and got a job as a tinsmith at a hardware store, making and repairing things out of galvanized sheet metal and solder. Then, after a few weeks, he moved on and got as far as Colorado before a continuing long-distance correspondence with a young woman back in Defiance pulled him back home. The young woman was named Cynthia, and I personally came to know her—many years later—as Grandma Mallett. Sometime when, as a kid, I forgot something, and had to go back to get it, he would comment "What you can't keep in your head you have to take out in your heels." In these days, his comment comes to my mind almost daily.

I remember my Grandpa Greenler as a retired farmer in Holgate, Ohio, who found many things to laugh about. He taught us grandkids how to play Euchre with him and my uncles, and he had comments to fit every happening in the game. For example, if you didn't have enough trump cards to take the required number of tricks he might say, "Looks like you ran out of soap before the washing was done!" or when he couldn't take an easy trick because he had only low cards, "I couldn't stop a hog in an alley."—and we'd laugh. The name Greenler was once spelled with the German umlaut ü rather than an ee, so I was aware of the German connection when he told his story about the "German guy" who liked his beer but was always eager to see a good street fight. At one time this guy had just gotten a beer served to him when a fight broke out just outside the bar. He figured that he couldn't take the beer into the crowd, but he didn't want to leave it, and then he had a bright idea: He scribbled on a napkin "I spit in this beer!", propped it up on the beer mug, and rushed out to see the fight. When he returned, he was glad to see his mug still there, full of beer—until he noticed that someone had added a note to the napkin "So did I."

There may well come a time when you have grandchildren, and

you might tell them about your Grandbob, and you might even give them a copy of this letter that you saved over the years. Of course, I would be their Great Great Grandbob.

So I hope this letter might be a direct message to people whom you will know well. Your direct and significant personal connections may well span five generations and this letter will extend a faint connection of another two generations. I'll end this epistle with a direct message to your grandchildren.

To the grandchildren of Skye and Ellie, Alex and Corry, Scott and Tommy:

By the time you receive this letter I will be long gone. But I want you to know that *this set of your grandparents* is a remarkable group. They grew up in close contact with each other and, in significant ways, are more like siblings than cousins. They have diverse interests and talents. I think each has a drive to follow his or her dreams and is motivated to do some Good in this world. I hope that you have similar drives, which will lead you to full rewarding lives. And I hope you feel as beloved by them as they are beloved by me. My best wishes to you!

Robert Greenler (2019)

First Communication

I've learned a lot from my children over the years.

Our little boy, Lee, was still a few weeks shy of attaining the milestone age of two. He had his vocabulary, of course, names for mother and father, probably aunts and uncles—I don't really remember the details these many years later. And he did have his own tools of communication that didn't require words: There was no doubt of his need for food, or his discomfort when touched with the tip of the diaper's safety pin, or his pleasure when riding his father's foot to the chant

> *Ride a cockhorse to Banbury Cross.*
> *To see a fine lady upon a white horse,*
> *Rings on her fingers and bells on her toes,*
> *And she shall have music wherever she goes.*

...followed by a *Whoops!* and a little toss in the air—repeated, by request, again and again. But he really wasn't into philosophical discussions.

In early spring a friend offered to let us live in an old farmhouse in the country, and we were excited to leave our small city apartment in Baltimore and spend a beautiful Maryland springtime in the woods, before making the next career move to Wisconsin.

One morning, as we were lingering over coffee at the breakfast table in the kitchen, Lee came toddling at top speed in from the living room, face flushed in excitement, shouting "Boppie! Boppie! Boppie!" It was not a word in our shared vocabulary, but we followed his urgent leading to the low window in the living room where, on the ground, just at the bottom of the window, lay a small, brilliantly colored bird. It was a beautiful indigo bunting, which had apparently flown into the window. We assumed that Lee had heard the thump on the window, seen the bird fall to the ground, and felt the need to report the remarkable event. He needed a word! Apparently, he associated this flying creature with others we had seen pecking for worms on the lawn or perching on our back-yard fence in the city, which we described with some word starting with a "b" sound. It probably was birdie, but in translation it came out boppie.

It was the first time that Lee had brought us word of news from the outside world—something that *he knew, and we didn't.*

A Day at Horicon Marsh

Early 1960s

It happened that the 30th of May was a beautiful spring day. It also happened to be our wedding anniversary. We decided to take the canoe, which Barbara and I had given to each other as our mutual wedding gift, to Horicon Marsh for an outing with our three small children. It was such a successful adventure that the following year—and years—our kids assumed that what we do on our wedding anniversary is to canoe in Horicon Marsh.

Those days all seem to blend into one day in my 60-year-old memory file. It involves launching our canoe and quietly moving away from the every-day routine of planning and doing and fixing and coping into a different world. It involved paddling to an island and unpacking the picnic hamper for a lunch surrounded by waterfowl and birdsong.

One of those years when we were there, I remember how our quiet lunch was interrupted with an explosive episode. It begins as the distant whine of a high-powered speedboat and develops as

eeeeeeeeEEEOWWWWWWWAAAAAAAaaooooooeeeeeeeeee.

At the screaming apex of this sound, the boat raced by the little island and left great waves pounding our small refuge. It probably took only a few minutes for the sound to pass beyond our hearing, for the waves to diminish and disappear, and for the birds to decorate the ensuing silence with their songs again.

Sobered, we talked about what a different experience it would be to be moving with that roaring chaos. Sometimes I think of the similarity of this little drama to the big picture of how we live our lives. Most of us spend some time traveling with the sound and chaos—and excitement—of the speedboat passengers. Some of us value being able to spend periods of time in that different world—after the speedboat moves on.

Ring Around the Rosie

After I finished graduate school in 1957, we moved to West Allis, Wisconsin where I worked in the research laboratories of the Allis Chalmers company. We rented a flat, which in Wisconsin means an apartment on the second floor of a house. The first floor was occupied by a middle-aged couple, who had no children. A year later our son, Lee, was three years old and his little sister, Karen, was nearly two. Then, on a Sunday afternoon, we had a rousing game of Ring Around the Rosie. I have no recollection of where we came across that game, and I assume that our version was at least partly homemade. We all joined hands, supporting little Karen, and danced in a circle, singing

Ring around the rosie.
Pocket full of posie,
Ashes, ashes,
All fall down.

We all laughed, dropping to the floor as we sang the last line. The merriment was increased by the mutual tickling that took place. It was great fun, so we did it again. But this time our little game was interrupted by a banging on the ceiling of the apartment below. We were making too much noise for the comfort of our downstairs neighbors. We stopped playing—our mood quickly changing. Before the hour was up, we decided that we needed to move to a more child-friendly place. Within the next week we came up with the possibility of renting an old farmhouse in the adjacent incorporated township of

New Berlin. It seemed like a great idea to me. Barbara had no experience in rural living but was willing to give it a try. We moved in and liked it so much that five years later we bought an old farmhouse north of Milwaukee. The house we left was shortly after burned down as a training exercise for the local fire department. The house we bought was in worse shape than the one we left, but over the next few years we fixed it up to fit our fancy and enjoyed living there for the next 44 years.

In 1971 I started a sabbatical year at the University of East Anglia in Norwich, England. During that year Karen, Lee, and I went to a theater production of a play about the bubonic plague that spread through the populated world in the mid- 1300s. It is estimated to have killed between one-third to two-thirds of the population of Europe over a five-year period. One of the incidents in this grisly tale was an explanation of the children's game, "Ring Around the Rosie," where it was pointed out that the ring referred to the circular red rash that appeared on the body of a person infected with the plague. "Pocket full of posie" describes the asafetida bag, a collection of herbs a person wore to ward off the petulance. "Ashes, ashes" evolved from "achoo, achoo", the racking cough that preceded the death…"All fall down."

We were shocked.

Something I Almost Didn't Do

Dawn was a tall, attractive undergraduate student who worked part time in the Physics Department Office at the University of Wisconsin-Milwaukee where I was employed. One day she came in wearing a tee shirt with the words "Long-stemmed American Beauty", illustrated by a single rose on a long stem. I commented on her neat shirt, and she said that she had gotten it from her father. I added that I had a daughter for whom such a shirt would be appropriate, and she said that her father, who lived in California, could get one for me.

I'm not sure exactly how I responded but expressed the concern that it would be an imposition on him. She insisted that he would be glad to do it and, although I had some misgivings, I thanked her and said that she might mention it to him—and if he did get it, I, of course, would pay for it. I added that my daughter, Robin, was about the same size as she, so, if her father really didn't mind, he would know what size to get.

A couple of weeks later, Dawn appeared pleased when she presented me with the new shirt—and Robin seemed pleased to get it. It was only years later that I heard the rest of the story. At the time of the gift, Robin had completed a growth spurt that made her taller than most of the girls—and even the boys—in her class at school. Naturally enough she felt awkward about it. And she told me that this was the first hint she had of thinking that her height might be a positive attribute, rather than an embarrassment—and I thought how close I had come to not following through with what just seemed like a good idea at the time.

A Dissatisfied Student

Daughter Karen went to the same school system, as did her older brother and younger sister, in the community near Milwaukee where we lived. It was considered to be a good system, but even good schools have some poor teachers. Lee and Robin probably had a similar assortment of teachers, but they reacted differently to the poor ones than did Karen.

Karen resented the arbitrary and sometimes hurtful rules imposed by people in charge; she labeled such rules as "Mickey Mouse". I worried that sometimes she was quick with the label for things she did not understand; however, there were times when I shared her resentment. One stands out in my memory.

As a result of some small infraction of the rules (which I do not remember) she was sentenced, as punishment, to write a 500-word theme. What a message that was—writing as a punishment! She grumped around and decided that she would write it on something disgusting and decided it would be on rats; that would probably gross out the teacher.

In that pre-computer age, she turned to encyclopedias and looked up material on rats. She actually got quite interested in the way several species of rats were transported from their native territories by the sailing ships that traversed all the seas of the world, taking them to new places where they wreaked havoc on local populations of animals and carried diseases affecting both animals and people. She composed her piece, wrote it up longhand, and gave it to the teacher. The next step was the real stopper: She watched him flip through the pages to see that she had met (even exceeded) the required word count—and tossed it onto his desk where she assumed that he would not bother to read it!

Karen's siblings were able to shrug off the failings of the occasional poor teacher, but she was not. We saw her turned off of one subject after another in the first two years of high school and decided that something had to change. She later described the time as a sliding into a depression, being without the ability to control any part of her life—probably caused by more than just hating school.

My parents were both schoolteachers and they believed that the public schools were one of the great features of our society; it gave children a chance to be educated—independent of their social status or financial resources. I think they would have had a moral objection to sending a student to a private school— and, to some extent, I inherited this attitude. This prejudice was challenged when I was living in Baltimore. While I was a graduate student, Barbara and I were married and we had our first child. We had friends who enrolled their children in private schools. Their impression was that in the 1950s the Maryland public school system was not uniformly of high quality, and the education of their children was too important to leave to the local public school. We understood this argument and now agreed that, whether our kids' school was good, fair, or poor, it wasn't a good place for Karen.

What could we do? Some friends had children at an alternative high school located 70 miles north of Milwaukee. It was described as a nonsectarian, coeducational, college-preparatory, boarding school. The school had a required core curriculum but offered students a considerable variety of choices to fill out their course schedule. Once they designed their schedule, they were asked to pledge to meet the goals they proposed.

Karen was enthusiastic to give it a try, and we agreed. She skipped some subjects that didn't interest her (e.g., mathematics) but entered fully into this new educational adventure. She made good friends and frequently brought one or more home for weekend visits. What Barbara and I saw was a life transformed. She developed a new appreciation for scholarship in a wide range of fields. Later, on her own, she worked through textbooks of the high-school and college math courses she had bypassed.

She spent much of her career at a small state university campus, dealing with students, many of whom, for a wide variety of reasons, had dropped out of the educational system and were taking tentative steps to restart it at the college level. She has helped many students rethink their educational goals and redirect their lives. No doubt her high school experiences gave her insight and inspiration to deal with these individuals.

I gained a great respect for the important role played by the smaller state university campuses and by the two-year campuses. I still believe strongly in a good public school system, but I see the life-changing role played by a private, alternative school in the life of this one, once-dissatisfied student.

The Farmhouse, the Barn, and the Playhouse

The Farmhouse.

Some of the important developments in my life are planned but many are the unintended side effects of the planning for other things.

In 1963 we bought an old farmhouse and barn with a variety of outbuildings on nine acres of land near Cedarburg, Wisconsin. The old farmhouse was a wreck; cardboard covered broken windows and the kitchen sink drained into an old diaper pail. Just across the drive from the front door was the dump where things that were no longed needed elsewhere were flung. The house suffered from neglect and poverty. Over the next few years, we renewed it and made it into the much-loved, comfortable farmhouse, where we lived for the next 39 years.

The Barn.

The barn was one of about a dozen octagonal barns built in Ozaukee County along the Lake Michigan shore by the Clausing brothers in the 1890s. It was one of four or five remaining barns and was something of a historical landmark, but it also suffered from neglect. The roof leaked and let water into the hay stored on the main floor. The wet hay was causing the floor and one of the main beams supporting it to rot. The water had also gotten into the fieldstone foundation, which was beginning to crumble. It was a critical time for the barn. We either had to fix it up or tear it down. Untended, it would soon be a hazardous place for curious children—or adults.

Although it was a bit of a financial strain for us, we decided to fix it up. To help the barn support itself (pun intended) the hay floor provided shelter during the winter months for boats. The boats had to be removed in the spring, and it provided a wonderful place for two weddings in our family and another for friends. Even during the winter, we usually managed to keep a path clear for a giant swing event. Inside the barn was a small granary room covered by a slanting roof. An adventurous child or adult could climb to the roof of the granary. He or she could be handed the end of a long rope suspended from the peak of the roof and could very carefully put one foot in a loop at the end of the rope, and step off into the biggest swing of their lives.

So, saving the barn for its historic value was not a driving motivation for the decision, but saving the barn from its rapid slide into oblivion turned out to have significant consequences. It is now one of the two remaining Clausing barns—the other having been moved to the Old World Wisconsin Historical Site in Eagle, Wisconsin. And ours—known as the Frank Vocke Farm—is on the National Register of Historic Places.

The rundown state of things explains why we were able to buy the property for $17,000. Before we moved into the house, we had the lath and plaster removed from all the exterior walls. Inside we removed doors and widened the openings to make easy connections between the rooms. In the kitchen we installed an island, cabinets, and the biggest Thermopane window available. We could sit at the big elliptical kitchen table and look out at the stone smokehouse and what became the back yard. Through another window in the kitchen, we could see into the little greenhouse, repurposed from being the mudroom in the old farmhouse. Then, with new drywall, wiring, and plumbing, we moved into what to us was our very comfortable farmhouse home.

A few years later, after a heavy snowfall, the overloaded roof on a machine shed attached to the barn collapsed. It was one more thing that needed attention. The old red-painted shed boards were still solid and the structural 2x4s (which actually measured 2" x 4") were sound. If I could get those weathered barn boards to someplace in New York City they would be worth big bucks—but I had no such connection. The solution to that problem came in the person of a friend, Chuck, who was one of the early members of the Nightingales Singing Group started by Barbara and two women friends. Chuck was in Milwaukee, with no job at the time, so I hired him to clean up the mess, salvaging the best of the barn boards and 2x4s and, of course, putting them in the barn, where there was always space for one more thing. So, it happened that I had—there in the barn—a bunch of old lumber and even a few packs of shingles left over from reroofing the barn.

Most projects start with an idea and then move on to acquiring the materials to build it. The playhouse started in a different way.

The Playhouse.

One day while idly thinking about what I could do with those old boards (probably avoiding some other task that I didn't want to do) the idea of a little house—a playhouse for my six grandkids—came to mind.

That seemed like a good idea. No doubt I sketched it out but I decided just to put together a simple structure. I knew how little kids like to get into a small space—a space too small for an adult is the best. So I decided that a little rectangular building with a shed roof, too low to enable an adult to stand up, would be just the ticket. On the high side of little building was an open doorway and a window opening, with additional window openings on each end. I built it to sit on concrete blocks at each corner—built it quickly with no great effort and with no thought of posterity. I do recall that it was a success with the grandkids. It was a house, a fort, or a hide-a-way. One of the favorites was when it was a fast-food place where someone would roar up on an imaginary motorcycle, buy imaginary food at the take-out window, and pay imaginary money before roaring off.

Another piece of the playhouse story came from the Science Bag programs that I was organizing at the University. In one of them "Why Does A Spinning Top Stop?" I wanted to explain one of Newton's Laws to people who were frightened by equations.

The equation in words is force = mass x acceleration. I wanted to get across the idea that if you applied the same force to two objects with different masses (weights) the heavier one would have a smaller acceleration than the lighter one. So I rigged two wires across the width of the lecture room. I had a long block of wood suspended from each wire with a couple of screw eyes. One was significantly longer than the other. I described them as rockets that were powered by identical little CO_2

cylinders, which could be set off by driving a nail into the end of the cylinder with the tap of a hammer. My assistant, Kurt, and I positioned our hammers and the audience picked up the countdown: 10, 9, 8…3, 2, 1, launch! Off they went—with an impressive noise—and shot across the room. Clearly the lighter one hit the far wall sooner than the other and the audience loved it.

Of course, this had nothing to do with the concept of a playhouse—except for the idea that I could fasten one of those wires to the playhouse with the other end attached to a tree some distance away. Important Messages could be launched and sent to a Secret Destination some distance away, barely visible through the trees and bushes.

So that's how the playhouse happened; something that resulted from a long line of unlikely events.

Part Two:

Influence of My Parents

Beekeeping

My father was a teacher. He started keeping bees when he was a young unmarried man. What started as a hobby expanded to an enterprise that involved 200 colonies of bees located in ten different locations. It became a part time job, with most of the work required in the summer—which fit well for a teacher who was not teaching in the summer.

The production of honey was considered a farming operation, and there was special permission for farm kids to get a driver's license at an early age for work connected with farming. I got a farm permit at age 14, so that I could take the trailer and get a load of supers (boxes of empty combs) from a storage area while dad worked at the bee yard. I learned to do my half of the work. Sometimes we would both work on examining each colony together, responding to problems we found and giving them supers as needed. Sometimes it would go faster if he worked down one row of hives and I worked down another. Of course, if anything seemed amiss, we would discuss it and I would get the benefit of his years of learning about the lives of bees.

In the busiest part of the summer, we would spend two or three days each week tending the different bee yards. The operation involved a lot of car time together, and it felt like a shared enterprise. It is not surprising that after I was married with my own family, I kept two or three colonies of bees for the next 30-some years or that, later, each of my three kids had a go at beekeeping when they moved into old farmhouses like the one in which they had grown up.

Around many of the activities that we do repeatedly, we develop rituals. One of the rituals of this beekeeping activity was that when we went through Fremont—a small town on our route—we would stop for an ice cream cone at our favorite place. If, on some day, we went through that same town twice, we would get cones twice that day. It was what we did.

There was another ritual that was less trivial than that one (though I still love ice cream), and that has influenced my way of looking at the world. It was the walk in the nearby area—particularly in the woods where one of the bee yards was located. After we finished the work in that location, we would look around to see what we could find of interest—and it seems there were always interesting things. In the spring we might find morels to take home, where mother would treat them as a celebration of spring as she fried them in butter, even if it yielded only a taste for each of us in the family. Or there might be sweet wild strawberries, or wildflowers that would survive the trip home if wrapped in a wet cloth. If we were very busy and had tasks that needed to get done at other bee yards, we might make a shorter trip around the woods, but the ritual was that we didn't skip it.

I remember one walk when we spooked a rabbit out of his hiding place in a pile of brush and watched carefully to see where he went next. We followed him from place to place until he returned to the brush pile where we originally found him. My father suggested that his behavior might indicate that he didn't just run and look for a place to hide, but had a system of refuges all figured out.

On one summer day, at that bee yard in the woods, we found the bees were gentle and easy to manipulate in the morning, but their behavior changed abruptly at midday. The hum of the hive was different, the rapid hovering flight of the bees around us indicated annoyance, and we got stung more often as we checked out the colony. This behavior is familiar to beekeepers and understood at one level. The bees that guard a colony are the same ones that gather nectar. When they are busy gathering nectar, they are contented and easy to handle. If it is rainy or dark when they are confined to the hive, they go into the defensive/protective mode. Woe be it to a potential poacher, who thinks that nighttime might be a good time to slip in and take a few frames of honey.

But this defensive behavior was what we were seeing on this early afternoon. My father connected this behavior to another of his observations: in the morning there was a local plant called smartweed, or knotweed, that was abuzz with nectar gatherers, but this activity ceased at about noon when, apparently, the flowers quit producing nectar and the bees returned to the hive, in a bad mood.

We knew of one situation where night-time raids on the hive were successful. Occasionally we would find a beehive with many scratch marks on the hive entrance. When this had happened recently, my father—with his sense of smell, much more acute than mine—could detect the odor of skunk. Apparently, this animal could somehow manage to eat a bee without getting stung on the tongue or in the gullet. The skunk would scratch at the entrance and lap up the tasty bees as they walked out to investigate the disturbance. This surmise was supported by finding the dried remains of bees in the skunk's scat. On rare occasions, this predation so seriously depleted the population of a particular hive that we had to trap the bee-eater and take him to a new place to live.

We speculated on things that we saw and looked for the implication behind the observation. There were a few small juniper bushes near one of our bee yards. My father observed that they had been about the same size for the past 20 years and speculated on whether it had to do with the sheep that were occasionally let into the area to graze. The sheep didn't seem to like the juniper, but they were not above trying a taste, just to be sure they didn't like it.

After a winter with heavy snow my father pointed out a bush with some of the bark chewed off. But the bark was only gone from the top part of the bush: in fact, the bark damage was bounded by a rounded surface sloping through the bush. He realized that the rabbits would only eat on the branches that extended up above the snow surface. And with that boundary, we could see the shape of that snow drift through the bush, in the hungry part of the winter, as clearly as if we had been there.

These, and other, observations began a life-long habit of mine. It prompted a dedication in my first book *Rainbows, Halos, and Glories.*

> *Dallas Greenler helped me to view the world with an inquiring mind. John Strong helped me develop the tools of science, to enhance my perception of the world. To them, who taught me the pleasures of seeing with the mind as well as the eye, I dedicate this book.*

My Mother's Speech

My mother was a kind, outgoing woman, whose speech patterns never included any profanity or even mild vulgarity.

One evening, the family was playing Anagrams, a kind of free-form Scrabble. When it was mother's turn, she had four letters spread out in front of her: f, a, r, and t. A long pause was broken as we kids began to giggle at her hesitation to make the obvious play. The giggling gave way to laughter, morphing into helpless tearful laughter as she refused to compromise. In her embarrassment, she could not see the alternate possibilities: *raft, far, fat, tar, rat,* or even *at,* and so she passed her turn, as one must do, when he or she *cannot* make any play.

She often quoted bits of poetry, often doggerel. She enjoyed colloquial verse such as James Whitcomb Riley's "When the Frost is on the Punkin". One snippet of rhyme that came up every now and then was a quatrain:

What a wonderful bird is the pelican,
His bill can hold more that his bellican.
He can hold in his beak
Enough food for a week.

It was not until some years later, when I had moved out into the wide, wicked world, that I discovered that these were really the first four lines of a limerick, written by Dixon Lanier Merritt (but often misattributed to Ogden Nash). The fifth line is: *But I'm damned if I see how the helican!*

My Father—Stretching the Limits

2020

My father's mobility became limited by problems resulting from many years of diabetes, and it fell to my mother to do all of the driving. She was a timid driver but did what was necessary. They came to visit us a couple of times a year when we lived in the old farmhouse in Wisconsin. The house was a half-mile from the Milwaukee River and was surrounded by cornfields, but I discovered that, with my Farmall Cub tractor, I could make my way along the edge of the cornfield and follow the farmer's tractor paths to the woods along the river and through the woods to the river edge.

Somewhere I found a seat from an old Jeep and, with some angle-iron braces, devised a way to mount it near the tractor seat, and I added a seat belt. It took some handling to get dad up on a box from which he could be maneuvered into the seat. He was willing to endure whatever contortions it took to get there, and, that accomplished, off we'd go. When we got to the woods, we'd stop and let the silence surround us—silence at first, but then we'd hear a bird singing, and perhaps be scolded by a squirrel challenging our presence in his territory, or hear the rustle of branches moved by a light breeze. Depending on the season we could see the spring flowers, or the goldenrod, or the colored leaves of the trees.

At the river's edge we might see ducks, or a muskrat, or a blue heron. It was a treat for us both and we were able to share something that he could not get in the other parts of his life. The effort involved—by both of us—in stretching the limits of what he could do was certainly justified by the result.

Later his mobility was further limited by having a foot removed—another result of the diabetes. He could, however, walk short distances with an artificial foot. I told my parents that I could take a week vacation, and by adding the two weekends we would have time for a nine-day trip. I offered to drive them anywhere they wanted to go. After thinking about it, they decided their choice was to make a trip around Lake Superior.

We headed to northern Wisconsin, crossed over into Minnesota at Duluth, and followed the road, which for long stretches ran just along water off the north shore of Lake Superior. At that time the road was not busy, and it provided wonderful views of the lake and the northern forests as we drove the 150 miles to the Canadian border at Grand Portage, near Thunder Bay, in Ontario.

Old friend Steve Krasemann had told me stories of the availability of wooded land parcels, available in Ontario—at that time—at ridiculously low prices. So, after we crossed the border, we decided to look around to see what we could find. This area would be about a 600-mile drive from Milwaukee and could be a possible vacation retreat. We talked with a couple of district clerks, who knew most of the residents in their area and received information to the effect that Ed or George might have a piece he would be willing to sell, and we got maps showing where the parcels were. We went on poor roads or tractor paths where the car got scratched up by the brush and we had trouble with muddy spots, and we saw some interesting possibilities. We went into places that mother would never have ventured into by herself but was totally relaxed in being a passenger with me driving. She said to me, "If we get stuck, I know you'll figure out how to get out." Dad loved the adventure. For him it stretched the limits imposed by his physical infirmities.

When we got to Sault Ste. Marie, we found that by piecing together two or three train rides, we could make our way up north through the beautiful Canadian wilderness to the little town of Moosonee. The village is located at the mouth of the Moose River where it enters the lower tip of James Bay. Moosonee had a population of less than 2,000 people, of which about 85% were Cree. Apparently, one can no longer make that trip from Sault Ste. Marie by train.

One of the stops en route was a place with no station platform. The ground was too great a distance from the lower step for Dad to negotiate. He was determined to get off and look around the area. We travelled with a folding wheelchair, but the long step down to the ground was a problem. He urged me to help him sit down on the top step so that he could go down, a step at a time, on his butt. He was willing to stretch the limits of his disability and not be deterred by any sense of public dignity.

In Moosonee, we looked over the interesting village and retired to the local hotel for the night. In the morning, we explored the possibility of getting down to the Moose River, where there was a dock for a boat that would take us up James Bay on a 12-mile run to where it widened out to become the great Hudson Bay. We were following, upstream, the historic route by which this part of Canada was explored, originally by fur traders and later by European immigrants settling in this New World. Getting down to the river was a problem; it was a long way down! The "stairs" were like the ones we sometimes see in parks: each step was formed by something like a railroad tie, backed up by 3 or 4 feet of dirt. I could ease the wheelchair down the step, which was usually barely wide enough to hold all four of the wheels— before the next step. As we started the process, people quickly stepped forward who were able and eager to help—one on each side of the chair—going down the long flight. At the end of the stairs, there was no gangplank access to the boat; one had to make a big step over the boat railing down onto the deck. With the number of helpers gathered around, there was no problem as willing hands gently lifted the chair, with my dad in it, onto the deck.

The details of the trip have dimmed in my mind, but two impressions remain very clear. I think of the many people, strangers, all along the way, who saw what was going on and wanted to help; and I think of my father, a gentle and unassuming man, who was willing to accept their help—to stretch the limits of what he could do. And as I sit describing it, these many years later, tears come to my eyes.

We didn't get serious about a land purchase at the west end of Lake Superior; our explorations there were something of an excuse for an adventure, but as we arrived at the Sault, at the east end of the lake, I thought again about acquiring a piece of land in that area. It could be nearer to 500 miles from home and might be within driving distance of our very close friends, Ray and Ellie Newell, who lived in Rochester, New York. We got together with them two or three times a year, and as our children were growing up, we camped with them in Michigan's Upper Peninsula or in Ontario. After that trip with my parents, I talked with Ray about the possibility of acquiring a piece of land and he immediately expressed interest. Over the next couple of years our search resulted in the purchase of an 80-acre piece of woodland near Thessalon (for the price to $700 Canadian). We camped on the land for a few years before building a cabin, which became the center of our contact with the Newells and of many vacations over the next decades.

Dad took great interest in our plans for building a primitive cabin on the property, but he died the year we started the construction. I regretted the timing. We would have worked out some way to get him back along the quarter-mile path from the gravel road to the cabin site, and he would have sat on the porch, viewing this precious spot in the world, and he would have loved being there.

Part Three:
My Growing Up

Staying Up Late

My parents are gone for the evening, and my two older sisters and I are on our own. We decide to play hide-and-go-seek, but there are not many good hiding places in a house where you have lived for several years. To make a game of it, we do it in the dark. With no streetlights in the small town, it really is quite dark and so touch and hearing are the things you have to use. Sometimes I can trick my sisters into a giggle with one of my "Bobby's smart-aleck" remarks, which gives away their location. It's always worth a try when I am "It". When I get close close enough in the quiet dark, I can hear them breathing.

In the kitchen my mother has a big wooden table where she rolls out the dough for making apple dumplings, or pounds the steak to make it more tender, and does all the stuff that mothers do to feed us. There are lots of things stored on the floor beneath the table and I think one of my sisters might be hiding back there among the clutter. I'm on my hands and knees, cautiously feeling my way in the dark, when I touch a smooth, round melon. Actually, I know it is a citron, from which my mother plans to make some pickled preserves. I put my hand gently on it and am repulsed when my finger goes sticking into a soft rotten spot! I holler, crawl out from under the table, and get to the light switch. When the lights come on, the game switches from hide-and-seek to a laughing, finger-pointing game about Bobby who stuck his finger into a rotten citron! I didn't like that part of the game very much.

Our parents come home, and we put up the usual protests

when told it is time for us to go to bed. Can't we stay up for a little longer? Can't we? Can't we? They ignore this protest until, finally, they say that it is late and they are going to bed, and we can stay up as long as we want to.

Oh boy. Oh boy. We can stay up and play all night long! Great! What a good deal! How can we be so lucky on this night! What will we do now? ...Actually it seems too late to start a new game...and none of us comes up with any really good ideas... of things we really want to do...and it's not very long until we decide to slip up to our beds...verrry verry quietly...so we don't wake up our parents.

First Airplane Ride

When I was 5 or 6 years old we lived about 50 miles from the small town of Van Wert, Ohio. Van Wert was widely known for its peonies. Nearby were acres of peonies, and most of the houses in the town had peonies in their yards. When these plants were in full bloom the town had a Peony Festival celebration with all the activities that a small town could organize. We went to join the festival, and the one thing that I clearly remember from that trip is an airplane ride. Someone with a small airplane would take people up for a short ride for a modest fee. If it weren't a modest fee, our family would not have indulged, but my father and I took to the air and it was a magic experience.

Years later, when my children were small, I told the story of my first airplane ride, and somehow it got to turned in a Little Bobby story. The "Van Wert Peenie Festival" became a gag line when the rest of the family, including Barbara of course, would enjoy a session of "Let's hop on pop". One of the themes was that the Peenie Festival was so great that you had to see it from the air as well as on the ground. Oh well, no harm done, I've suffered worse.

Recently, while talking with my sister Phyllis I told her the story, which got me wondering what the actual facts are about this festival. On an impulse I typed into Google Search "van wert ohio peony festival". Lo and behold, there are pages of references to Van Wert and the festival! One of the sites summarizes the history:

Van Wert was known as the peony capital of the world in the early 1900s with many local gardeners growing fields of the flower. The first Sunday in June beginning in 1902 was designated as Peony Sunday.

The community held the first Peony Festival in 1932 and continued until 1960 with some missed years during World War II and the 1950s. In 1992, the Peony Festival returned and has been celebrated each year since its resurrection.

So, there it is, *famous the world over*! and I can say to my grown-up kids: "Nyah, nyah, nyah!"

Threshing Day

My Uncle Jake was a farmer in northwestern Ohio, married
to my mother's older sister, May. Aunt May died of a burst
appendix when I was three years old, so I have few memories of
her. My uncle lived for another couple of decades, and I have
a number of memories of him and his farm. One memory is
sitting on Prince, one of his horses, while he was cultivating
corn. By my measure Price was gigantic, and I sat atop this
powerful beast as he marched between the rows. The horse collar
was tipped by two shiny brass balls, which I could grip with my
small hands to give me a sense of security while riding high in
the air, feeling like the King Of The Universe.

When I rode Prince in the cornfield, the team of Prince and
Rose were involved in many of the farming activities, but
suddenly, when farmers were able to buy tractors, horses were no
longer needed. Uncle Jake kept his team of horses even after he
got a tractor. I remember one of his friends joking that the only
time he ever used the horses was to pick up feed for them at the
feed mill. And, of course, he didn't even use them for that…but
they were a valued part of his family and deserving of a good
retirement.

My uncle also raised wheat, and the processing of a wheat crop
in those days was something that required more than the effort
of the individual farmer. As I remember, a dozen or so farmers
would join together to buy a giant threshing machine. Then
they and their hired men would make a circuit of the farms in
the threshing ring and provide the labor to thresh the wheat that

had been cut and shocked in the fields ahead of time. In the case of my uncle, it would be done in one long laborious day.

It was my good luck to be a part of this annual event in the summer of the mid-1930s. As I think about it now, I am impressed with all the logistics that must have been involved in the operation of the ring. Who goes first? How do the finances work out with farmers who have a bigger or smaller farm than the others? How far could they move this giant machine at the end of a day? But I was just a seven-year-old kid who, although I didn't live on a farm, was lucky enough to be there on the day when my uncle's wheat was threshed. I was of such an age that I had no duties. There were two other kids of my own age who were there, also with no duties, and I suppose with strict instructions to stay out of the way. We had a great time.

It was, to my eyes, a vast operation. Out in the fields men with pitchforks were tossing sheaves of wheat onto wagons, which were pulled by tractors (no horses this year) to the threshing machine where they stood in line, the drivers in turn pitching the sheaves onto the moving belt that fed the maw of the giant machine. They circled back to pick up another load while others waited in the line to collect the grain coming down a chute and take it to a granary or truck it to the mill. Another group organized the constant stream of straw that shot out of a long, dinosaur-like appendage to the threshing machine. The snout of this creature could be moved around—at the signals from a stacker—to build a straw stack that could be used over the rest of the year. It was a very large operation that involved dozens of men, tractors, wagons, trucks, and a great deal of noise.

Another sizable operation involved all of the women who were preparing food for this operation. I was not privy to most of their activity, but I remember the scene when the bell next to the farmhouse was rung. The deafening sound of the monster machine stopped, tractors went silent, and all the men trooped up to the house where a tub of water stood in the shade of the big tree just outside the kitchen. Men beat the dust from their clothes and washed hands, arms, heads, and hair in the tub, one after the other, and dried themselves on the towel. That done, they moved to a long table where, plate-by-plate, they consumed a mountain of food. After finishing with the main courses, they had their choices of a large assortment of pies that had come from the kitchens of all of the women involved. The men retired to sitting or lying on the ground, talking, laughing, and resting for a time before returning to—what seemed to me—the organized chaos of the threshing. As this threshing circus moved from farm to farm, the labor of the womenfolk, an essential part of the operation, was repeated day after day until the work was done.

My two friends and I stayed well enough out of the way, on that magic day, to avoid trouble. I remember that once my uncle stopped by to see what we were doing in the granary. He was a large heavy-set man with a twinkle in his eye. He looked us over, with his thumbs planted under his suspenders. He leaned back and proclaimed:

A boy's worth half a man,
Two boys, worth half a boy,
And three boys—worse than no boy at all.

And then he tipped his head back and laughed.

A Small Business in a Small Town

One summer day, when I was 8 or 9 years old, in the small Ohio town where I was growing up, I found a very big empty crate. It was behind some store, and I think it may have been used to ship a refrigerator. After determining that it was indeed trash, I managed—with the help of Jack and Ted, kids who lived across the street—to get it home, knowing that it could be used for something interesting.

The next day I decided that I could have a vegetable stand at the edge of the street, right by our house. We had plenty of fresh vegetables in the garden, so why not try selling some of them? From somewhere among her treasures, my mother came up with a roll of red, white, and blue bunting, which covered the front and sides of the crate when it was sitting on its long side. A perfect arrangement for selling some vegetables. When I got a couple bunches of carrots, some tomatoes, and squashes, I was in business.

Jack and Ted hung out with me some of the time, and I spent most of the day, sitting in the shade of the big maple trees that lined our street, waving at people in cars as they drove by, and talking to anybody walking down the sidewalk. By the end of the day, I had sold one bunch of carrots—and nothing else. Oh well, some ideas work out better than others. And it was not a bad way to spend a long summer day.

A few days later, my mother suggested that I might try selling some of the vegetables by putting them in my wagon and going around the town. On a Saturday morning she gathered a selection of vegetables and helped me arrange them in the wagon. She also suggested some people who might be interested in buying fresh vegetables.

That was the beginning of a regular Saturday morning routine for the rest of the summer. I developed a route with some regular customers. Mrs. Apt frequently took a bunch of carrots. Mrs. Schilling, at the hotel, would go for some acorn squash. Mrs. Beech, at the funeral home, would almost always take a quart of shelled lima beans. There was some effort in shelling the beans so that quart brought a good price.

My favorite customer was Mrs. Burgoyne, who always took a couple of summer squash. Her memory didn't seem to be very good, as she asked me on several visits how to cook them. I had been coached by my mother, so I explained to her how to cut them into small chunks, put them into a pan with a little water, cook them for a few minutes till they were tender, and then drain off the water and season them with butter and salt. She frequently offered me something cold to drink and I always liked to go into her house and see the interesting things she had picked up on trips to different places. I remember some time later when I received a coconut in the mail from Florida. Of course, I had seen coconuts before, but this one was in a big husk, which I had never seen, and it just came in the mail to me with an address label pasted right on the husk. It said TO: Bobby Greenler, FROM: E. Burgoyne. To me it was as exotic as if it had come from Mars. It was many years later when mother mentioned that Mrs. Burgoyne loved to hear me patiently explain to her how to cook summer squash.

I usually returned from my route around town with a nearly empty wagon. I hadn't thought, until I sat down to write this account, that someone must have been keeping track of what sold and what didn't, and probably listened to my reports of what people wanted that I didn't have so that I could expand my market.

With the money I made, we started a savings account at the bank—in my name.

What did I get from that summer's small-business experience? A number of things come to mind: learning to talk, and listen, to adults; taking responsibility; a relation between work and money; and a sense of self confidence. Perhaps the biggest lesson of all was learning how to be a good parent.

A Gift

I graduated from the sixth grade in the town of West Unity, a rural town of about a thousand people in the Northwestern corner of Ohio. In the fall I entered the seventh grade in Raymer Elementary School on the east side of the big city of Toledo, only 50 miles away from West Unity. Though it was only 50 miles, it was a foreign culture to me. I was familiar with kids getting into wrestling matches at recess time, but not in fights where some kids would even try to hurt one another. Everything was different in the big city, and I had no friends.

One day I was walking home from school and fell in beside a classmate, whose name was Harold. I found out that he was not going home but was going to the library. "A Library? Where is it?" "It's nearby. You never been there? I'll show you where." Harold not only showed me where the library was but showed me how I could get a card that would let me borrow *any number of books*—for free! I remember getting some books from a particular shelf—the second shelf from the floor. They were so good that I decided I would just start from the left end of the shelf and read all of the books in order.

I can't remember the name of any of the books on that low shelf, nor do I have any idea of the classification of that section of the library's collection. But I remember that it was a new world to a kid who needed to find a new world in his life.

I didn't have a particular friendship with Harold, and I don't remember if we were even in the same high school, two years later. But, on that fall day, he gave me a gift that influenced the rest of my life.

Write it Down!

In my high school, almost every hall locker sported a combination lock. A friend of mine apparently had two combination locks, one of which she put in a drawer until she forgot the combination. When Jeannie commented that she would have to throw it out, I asked if I could work on it. Of course, she agreed, having nothing to lose.

So, I decided to see what I could learn about such a lock. The front of the lock showed a dial with numbers on it, which you could turn with the central knob. The back of the case was a metal disc, held securely in place by the rolled-down edge of the steel case. There was no obvious way to free the back, but I found that if I applied enough force with a small chisel, I could pry up a short section of the rolled-down edge. It took a long time to pry around the edge until I could finally remove the back—and could view the insides of the lock mechanism!

Now is the time, I fear, to say farewell to the reader who has no interest in the machinations of a teenager who is excited by being able to claw his way into the vitals of a combination lock. Is this bizarre interest the result of the kid's Nature or Nurture? Who knows? And who cares? I was about to understand something I did not know, and the excitement was that of solving a puzzle—with no thought of any practical application.

Inside I find three metal discs, all the same size, spaced with washers along the metal shaft connected to the front dial. When the dial is turned only that first disc rotates. But there is a tooth on that disc that can push against a similar tooth on the second disc, so it will turn along with the first—and a tooth on the other side of that disc that can push against the tooth on the third disc. So, if the knob is turned a couple of turns to the left, each of the teeth will be pushing against the next and the discs will be turning together.

Take a deep breath if you are still with me. On the edge of each disc there is a notch, and the key to the lock (so to speak) is what happens when these three notches all line up together. When they all line up, in the right position, a lever can rotate into the notches and the other end of that lever releases the hasp of the lock and allows it to be pulled out of the lock body. Voila!

One last step and the mystery of the combination padlock is solved. Spin the dial a couple turns to the left and turn the dial to the point where the notch of the first disc is in the appropriate place and **write down that number**! That is the first number of the combination. Then turn the dial to the right until the notch in the second disc is in the appropriate place and **write down that number.** That is the second number of the combination. Then rotate the dial to the left until the notch on the third disc matches that of the others and **write down that number**—the third number of the combination that opens the lock.

I emphasize the writing down of the newly discovered key to the lock. What comes to mind is an expression of a friend who misquoted a platitude, saying "The strongest mind is weaker than the palest ink", which translates as "**Write it down!**"

I pounded down the segments of the previously rolled-down

edge and returned the lock—and the piece of paper with the combination—to my friend, who thanked me for all of my efforts. Her thanks were the lesser portion of my reward. The greater portion was the satisfaction of solving an interesting puzzle.

Now, to any of you readers who have persisted to this point, and whose attention spans I have not exceeded, I offer you the second chapter of "My Career as a Locksmith".

Several decades later, I was sitting at one of my favorite places on this earth: A primitive cabin at the end of a quarter-mile-long walking path. The other end of the path is hidden from the view of anyone driving down the gravel road, which comes off a highway a couple of miles from the town of Thessalon in the Province of Ontario. My family and I, along with the family of my long-time friend, Ray, had designed and built this cabin, lovingly, with hand tools. It was a vacation haven where I relaxed, both physically and mentally.

We had built a small shed to house the cart we used to carry materials to build the cabin and the sleds we used to bring luggage and supplies from the road. It provided a storage place for tools and useful material that would not fit into the small cabin. The door to the shed was secured by a combination padlock, and **the combination was written down** in at least three places.

It is surprising to contemplate all the ideas that I've hatched, sitting on the porch of that cabin, unhindered by a to-do list. One afternoon, I sat with that padlock in hand and thought about my high-school experience with the-padlock-of-no-combination. As I thought through my discovery of the secrets of that padlock, a new insight sprang to mind. If, instead of starting the opening of the lock by turning the dial a couple of turns to the left, you started by spinning the dial to the right, there should be a different set of numbers that would open the lock. This would be a different set than was given to the new owner by the manufacturer, but there should be such a set for any such combination lock!

*Dear reader, I will not exhaust you with the ensuing details, but by guessing at the width of the teeth (as measured by numbers on the dial) I could deduce the combination. After a few guesses, I came up with the alternate combination that opened the lock. Nobody in my world had suggested the existence of such a thing, but **I had discovered it!** It induced the same pleasure of discovery as my solution of the lost-combination-puzzle of the distant high-school recollection. And in thinking about that episode, I also recalled a postscript to the earlier experience. I had written down the combination and given it to my friend along with the recommissioned lock. It was a few weeks later, while we were eating lunch in the school cafeteria, that she commented to me that she had apparently misplaced the paper on which I had written the combination, and wondered if I remembered what it was. I did not.*

A Trip to Remember

It was the week before spring break, and Dwayne and I discovered that neither of us had plans for the week off. I was a senior in high school and Dwayne a first year college student, and we had been close buddies for some years. We came up with the really good idea that, since neither of us had been as far away from home (Toledo, Ohio) as New York City—and we had a whole week—we could hitchhike there and back. Dwayne had a cousin in New York and was sure he would let us sleep on the floor of his apartment, so we wouldn't really need any money.

I told my parents what we planned to do, and it was clear that they were not as excited by the plan as we were—but they didn't say no, so the trip was on. My parents drove us from Toledo to an aunt and uncle's house east of Cleveland, 150 miles on our 600-mile trip to the Big City. The next morning they dropped us on the nearest big highway and we put out our thumbs, eagerly anticipating our adventure. By that night we had gotten rides that left us in Rochester, New York, by which time we had exhausted the food supplies tucked away in our small backpacks.

The details of the trip have diminished in my memory. We did ride the subway, see Central Park, visit Grant's tomb, and discover the Horn and Hardart automated cafeterias where you could get food out of coin-operated machines—a marvel that had not penetrated to the Midwest in 1947. Our meager funds stretched just enough to let us see a performance of the

Rockettes at Radio City Music Hall. We were amazed at the wonders we saw everywhere—as we went on our more-or-less random, three-day ramble around Manhattan.

We got back home without incident, and our arrival was celebrated in the family as a homecoming after a successful adventure. Some years later, after being seasoned by some of the realities of life, I asked my mother how she and dad felt about us going on that trip. She told me that she asked him "Can we possibly let them do this?" and he replied, "I don't see how we can possibly say 'No.'"

Tears come to my eyes as I recall that conversation. I marvel that they understood the significance of this adventure to me. Many parents would have said "No", and many children would have had to find other secret, more dangerous ways of "proving themselves" to be adults, but my parents were there to celebrate this Rite of Passage. I resolved, at that time, to have such understanding when my children were coming of age.

My UFO

Recent news stories stir my memory and bring up an incident that occurred seventy-some years ago.

One Saturday when I was a college student, living at home while working a summer job, I decided to construct a hot-air balloon. Using materials at hand, I pasted together a three-foot-diameter sphere of tissue paper and, at the bottom, formed a mouth with a ring of aluminum wire. The burner, which was to heat the air in the balloon, was a small wad of alcohol-soaked cotton in a piece of aluminum foil, held in the center of the ring with small wires. I had intended to launch it the next day, but some visiting friends of my parents were so intrigued to see it that we went with them to a park with a large grassy area, to launch it that evening.

As soon as I lit the alcohol burner, the bag plumped up into a rigid sphere, brilliantly illuminated from the internal flame. Released, it rose straight up—an impressive glowing, orange sphere in the dark night. It rose above the tree level of the nearby woods into a wind that moved it rapidly along—a magnificent sight as it was swept away downwind.

Apparently, the flame was too hot for the paper. When the paper ignited it was so hot that it burned in an instant and the wire frame dropped in the darkness. It was not until the next day that I started to think of how that incident might have appeared to a person driving his car along the nearby road. What that person "saw with his very own eyes" depends entirely on the *unconscious* assumption he made about how far away the balloon was. We get information with our binocular vision about the distance to nearby objects, but that depth perception would give no clue to an object as far away as the balloon. We do get an intuitive estimate of distance if we know the size of the object we are viewing—a car, for example—but here the object would not be recognizable.

So, if the fellow was driving down the road, two hundred feet from where I launched my three-foot balloon, and his *unconscious* impression was that this glowing sphere was a mile away, he would see it as an object 80 feet across; the size of a spacecraft! He would see it rise up until it abruptly changes direction and with an acceleration—unmatched by any of other spacecraft—travels at a very high speed for ten seconds or so, when it emits a brilliant flash and disappears. He wouldn't have believed it if he hadn't seen it with his very own eyes.

I watched the newspaper for a notice of a new UFO sighting, but none was reported. My imagination took me to a conversation with a "believer" who heard the detailed report from a reliable observer, complete with numerical estimates of size and speed. I might suggest that there are many possible explanations for such a sighting other than a secret government project or an alien spacecraft. "Such as?" "Well, such as a searchlight on a cloud layer…or a mirage effect from a car on another road, beyond the trees…or a kid launching a paper balloon." "Come on, be reasonable, those are the suggestions of a closed-minded skeptic, grasping at straws."

Me? I was just playing.

My Song-Writing Career

My interest in song writing began when I was in college. It was through my acquaintance with a talented musician, who was of my parents' generation. As a young woman in the 1920s, she had helped support herself in college by playing the piano at a silent-movie theater. Of course, she knew all of the popular tunes of that era and those of a few decades earlier. Even a generation later she could play an endless sequence of those tunes, shifting seamlessly from mood to mood as an imaginary silent movie worked through its plot. Later she was a violinist in the National Symphony Orchestra and was involved in many teaching activities with children, including preschool kids.

I say that Mrs. G was of my parents' generation. Actually, she was the mother of Mary, the girl I dated in those college years. Mary's younger sister, Betsy, was a preschooler. I enjoyed playing with Betsy, and after I wrote some simple poems about animals for her, Mrs. G. set them to music. Each poem suggested movements that a preschooler could do marching around the room while singing. They proved popular with Betsy and other children's groups that her mother instructed. An example:

"The elephant must surely be
My very biggest friend.
He looks so funny cause it seems
His tail is on the wrong end."

…sung as the kids march in a circle with one arm hanging over the head and swinging back and forth as they move in time to the music. Rich humor, it seems, for kids of a certain age. Or:

"Did you ever think
When you go to the zoo,
That the laughing hyena
Is laughing at…YOU!"

…when the last word is delayed, with excitement, to see who gets pointed to.

Buoyed by this success I submitted a few of the poems to the magazine *Highlights for Children*. They were published, and I was rewarded with small payment—a documented beginning of my song-writing career.

I tried to write a "popular" song of the times, and, of course, Mary's mother immediately put it to music. She suggested that we show it to one of her wide collection of musical acquaintances, one who had authored a number of commercially successful popular songs. A few evenings later, at his home, we chatted briefly and then Mrs. G sat at the piano and played through the music she had written to accompany my words of the song "Goodbyes". He commented that there were hints of a couple of great melodies in her piece that could be developed into songs. Then I gave him the paper with my words. I knew that there were some parts that hadn't yet gelled, but I thought there were some promising parts in it.

He started to read the first line aloud, slowly, and deliberately, word-by word, without any trace of expression:

"I'm getting tired of saying goodbye to you."
Pause…followed by his comment: *That stinks!*
Next line: "Saying goodbye won't satisfy me like it used to do."
That really stinks!!
Next lines:
"Sometime soon, I hope we'll find
that we have left goodbyes behind
and I can spend, begin, and end,
each day with you."

…all delivered in an expressionless, word-by-word monotone that could strip any writing of its grace.

I don't think he read, aloud, any further into the verse—and in fact I don't remember any more of the verse. He read the rest to himself and without further comment slapped the paper onto the table.

After what seemed like a very long, painful silence he moved to the piano and started to play a song, singing some lyrics to accompany it. He admitted that he was stuck on the next part and said that if I wanted to look at it, he would listen to my suggestions. If it worked out, and he used any of my ideas, he would thank me and never give any public recognition that I had anything to do with it. Take it or leave it.

I left it. I wanted nothing to do with such an unfeeling, insulting, egotistical character. I don't remember any more about how the evening ended. Sometime later I realized that in his own offensive way he was offering me a chance to take a first step into the song-writing business. He obviously had seen, in my flawed attempt, *something* that made him think I might have a suggestion worth hearing. If I passed this test, the next collaboration might have some little reward in it for me. But my pride was so offended that I was unwilling to grovel.

I had many other things going on in my life, and as it turned out, that was the end of my song-writing career—at least until now.

Firefighting

In my first year of college, I had a friend who was from Boise, Idaho. Bob knew about a small outfit in Idaho called the Southern Idaho Timber Association, and I—needing a summer job and looking forward to an adventure—wrote them a letter. It resulted in a job offer. When classes and exams were finished, we went to my home in Toledo, Ohio for a couple of days and then took off on a 40-hour bus trip to Boise. There we went our separate ways, and I caught another bus to a very small town 60 miles to the north. Smiths Ferry recently reports a population of 75 persons—probably slightly larger than it was when I arrived seventy-some years ago.

The Timber Association was a private group responsible for fire protection on a large spread of standing timber. It was served by two lookout towers that commanded the surrounding area. Observers on the lookout peaks could spot a source of smoke during the day or a fire at night. They each could determine an accurate azimuth angle to the fire from their positions. The intersection of those two lines-of-sight determined the precise location of the fire on a map. When this information was shared by radio, the stage was set.

The operation of the Timber Association no doubt resulted from geography and weather patterns of this particular area. With only one exception during my summer stay, the fires on "our land" were started by lightning strikes on local mountain peaks. The pattern was quite predictable. Sometimes in the early evening there were a few clouds appearing, resulting in a few lightening strokes, and nothing more. Occasionally one of these strokes would start a fire, and we would spring into action.

The only roads in the area were rough logging roads. Over the winter these roads would be blocked by small washouts. Most of our days were spent repairing the roads that gave us access to the area. At one time in the summer a group of half a dozen old guys joined us to rebuild some of the wooden bridges spanning the small creeks. These guys (sometimes referred to as woods bunnies) had spent most of their lives working in the woods and most were artists with the double bitted axes they used in their work.

In my naivety I assumed that those who spent their lifetime in the woods would hold it in some regard for its beauty. At lunch time, bags of food appeared from a kitchen somewhere, and most of us would find a log to lean against while we relaxed and ate the food provided. When we finished the respite and moved on, the site looked like a disaster area—with bags and paper plates and cups and napkins scattered everywhere. I was shocked. I slowly came to understand their attitude. This was a large, forested, uninhabited place which they viewed as an endless wood that, in time, would take care of itself. If they came back next year to this place, all of this stuff would be gone.

In rebuilding the short bridges, sometimes the work involved building the cribbing on either side of the stream. It was like building the side of a log cabin, but with corner angles being greater than 90 degrees. When it came time to notch one of these logs, the job might be done by whomever was working nearest that end of the log. I was very careful to be somewhere else, working with a shovel or pulling on a peavy to roll a log. I would watch the guy with the ax squint at the angle, cut a notch halfway through the log, and clear out the chips by twisting the ax with his last cut. Usually, the log would be rolled into place—fitting perfectly.

When a fire was started by lightning on a mountain peak on an evening when there was no wind, it would not spread. A fire on the side of a hill will burn uphill much more readily than downhill. The agent is the uphill draft caused by the fire. The usual pattern was that the fire would not spread until the morning breezes came into the picture. Having received the radio message from the towers and located the fire on our map, we would drive the logging roads to the nearest spot and take off uphill with headlamps lighting the way. If we could get to the fire before dawn, it could be handled by two or three of us. With shovels, axes, and a grub hoe, we could deal with a small fire.

The one exception to this way of dealing with fires in the forest under out jurisdiction was a fire that started on a road running through the valley, far below our forest. The assumption was that it was started by a carelessly discarded cigarette butt. The fire travelled uphill on a border of land that on one side was under the care of the state fire service and on the other side was a national forest that was the responsibility of the U.S. Forest service. The local management of these groups had the philosophy that it was dangerous to have their crews stumbling through the forest at night. They would see that their boys had a good breakfast before tackling the fire. By morning this fire had travelled the significant distance uphill to reach land that was under our protection. So, all three groups were involved in treating what could become a major fire. A bulldozer was brought in to help clear fire trenches to contain the blaze. Much hand labor was needed to complete the trenches that the bulldozer started. We were all alert to putting out small blazes started across the fire line by flaming debris carried aloft by the updraft of the fire.

Many of the details of the two or three days of that fire have escaped my memory. I remember being so exhausted that I was permitted lie down in the dirt of one of the fire breaks and catch a blessed short nap. One event still remains vivid in my mind. I was working in the fire trench near the bulldozer. The driver was clearing out some trees to widen the trench when, suddenly, the top of one of the large nearby trees erupted into flame, and a few seconds later the crown of an adjacent tree adjacent tree also flared up. The driver of the bulldozer, caught in the middle of this conflagration, leapt from his seat and ran to where we were—a very short distance downhill. The machine was engulfed in flame as we stood by helplessly. The dozer engine was running chug-a-chug-a-chug-a chug a CHUNK— as the cooling water ran out and the engine seized up. With the help of the big crews, that flare-up was confined to a fairly small area, and the larger fire was brought under control.

I completed the summer without any further excitement. I relished the weekends when, with no fire hazards, I could take a day's leave to wander about the mountains. On one Sunday, I got up before dawn to get into an area that I had not explored. As the day warmed I was pleased to find a mossy area where I lay down to rest—and fell soundly asleep. I woke up slowly and, without moving, became aware of a silence. There was no sound of traffic, no radio, no sound of a breeze, no sound of the clothing that accompanies any body motion...nothing. It was a silence that I had never before experienced. I listened some minutes until I detected—at a great distance, at the very edge of my hearing—the faint baying of a dog.

It was a great summer adventure that took a new twist as I packed my few belongings into my backpack, stood along the road, with my outstretched thumb, starting another adventure: hitchhiking back home.

The Trip Home

1948

It was getting along toward evening when the car stopped to pick me up. I didn't know how long this ride would last but I hoped it would be all night because I was eager to get home. Hitchhiking to Ohio after a summer job as a firefighter in Idaho was a long haul. But at that time, after my first year at college, a long time ago, it was also an adventure.

To the usual hitchhiker's question, "How far ya goin?" the man driving the car gave a vague answer. "I'm going a long way." It was not clear how far he was going, or how far he was going without stopping for some sleep. He seemed very preoccupied with some mission, and I soon found that asking direct questions didn't yield direct answers. What I was going to find out about this trip was what he decided to tell me—in his own good time.

The man didn't match any of the categories in my memory file. He was old, probably in his late forties. His face, seen in the lights of the approaching headlights, was gaunt and sallow. His thin gray hair was cut short and his speech seemed unremarkable, which no doubt meant he had a midwestern accent, similar to my own.

He was hesitant to tell me the story that was clearly behind this nocturnal trip, but it was also clear that he needed to tell it. The pieces of the story came out in a sort of random order. I settled in to listen, feeling no impatience with the process. If it took all night for him to tell his story, I would make good progress on my trip home. In my memory that night is a surreal happening involving two people, brought together by the luck of the hitchhiker.

"I'm driving to New York City," he said, "to make a collect telephone call—which should take no more than five minutes—and immediately start driving back to a small town in Indiana." Now I knew that he was going a long way in the direction I was traveling. Later he told me, "The most important thing in my life is a little girl who is four years old," and then he pulled a snapshot from his wallet and showed me what seemed to be a picture of an ordinary four-year-old girl, whom I later understood to be his daughter.

He resented a divorce arrangement that allowed him to take his daughter for a weekend only every other week, and he had filed a court action, in the Indiana town where his former wife lived, to get custody of the little girl.

The man, piloting us through the darkness, told me that he had given his lawyer directions. "I told him to follow my instructions exactly—with no deviation and no questions. He is to walk into the hearing room at exactly 11:30 on Friday morning, and is to have with him the papers that allow me to have my daughter that weekend." He had recently told his ex-wife that he was giving up the court action and going to Europe. To give credibility to his story he had let her see a passport among some of his papers. On Thursday, the day before the court hearing, he would place the collect telephone call to his ex-wife from New York City. In asking whether she would accept the long-distance charges, the telephone operator would provide the information that the call was from New York City, and during the call the man would say that he was just about to leave for Europe.

It was clear that he had run the Friday scenario through his mind time and time again and was convinced that it would work exactly as he planned. At precisely 11:30 in the morning, he would pull into town, go to the hearing room, and, since no one was there to contest his suit, would be awarded custody of his daughter. Then he and his lawyer would walk across the street and ask the sheriff to accompany them to the house where he could show his ex the necessary papers allowing him to take his daughter for the weekend. Before any further legal action could take place, they would use the plane tickets that were in his packed suitcase in the car trunk and fly to a place in Mexico (not disclosed to me—or anyone else I assumed) where they would start a new life.

For years after that I didn't tell anyone the story of that strange night. Did his scheme work? Are father and daughter living in happy seclusion in some out-of-the way place in Mexico? (That seems to be one of the least likely outcomes.) What effect did this scheme have on the lives of the little girl and her mother? Did my hearing that story somehow make me an accomplice in this bizarre plot?

This man was outside my experience. I was sympathetic to someone whose life was so dominated by his concern for his daughter, but appalled by his machinations to fix things as he would have them. I think that few situations other than the intimacy between strangers—resulting from this long trip together, in a car, through the dark night—would have caused him to share his story with me.

My involvement ended as we came into Fort Wayne. Perhaps the man decided that he had finished his story and needed to get some rest before getting on with his precisely scripted plan. He stopped a taxi and asked the driver the location of the nearest brothel. For a five-dollar tip, the cabbie led us through an alley, slowed down, and indicated the entrance to the place. Before returning to the alley, my driver took me back to a corner on the main highway where, with the sun brightening the eastern sky, and, as if emerging from a dream, I started looking for my next ride home.

A Canoe Trip

In the summer of 1950, I finished my summer job in a factory in Toledo, saving two weeks for an adventure with my friend Ray before going back to school. Ray and I had shared hiking, bird watching, and nature photography interests, but we had never canoed together. In fact, as far as I can remember, I had only been in a canoe a few times. That was about to change. I headed off to his home in Schenectady where we put together a set of camping gear and some food, put the canoe on top of the car, and headed north into Quebec. The canoe was one owned by Ray's older brother who had gone on a canoe trip with a friend in Quebec a few years earlier and had returned with a birchbark canoe.

After we passed through Ottawa, we got into a part of the country that was very sparsely populated. Late in the day, I recall stopping to ask an old man along the road where we could find a motel. He fit my mental classification of being an old geezer—perhaps as old as I am now. We asked the question a couple of times, but he didn't seem to understand what we wanted. Finally, the problem became clear when he shouted *"motel? motel?* Around here we call them *hotels!"* It was a sign of the times and of the locale.

We had researched the area we wanted to explore and gotten maps of the large LaVerendrye Wildlife Preserve. We put in at the north edge of this 5,000-square-mile wilderness area and headed south. We went up big rivers, across lakes large and small, and up little rivers until our way was blocked by the frequent beaver dams. Ray was a more-experienced canoeist than I, but we both learned by experience the things wilderness travelers soon know. For instance, if you are camping on a sand beach, you should never step across the area where you are cooking food, or soon every bite you take will have that gritty taste. We fished, struggled up-wind in the rain, drifted lazily down-stream in the sunshine, crept up close to see moose, and played with the local loon, trying to outguess where he would surface next.

The canoe served us well. We had to touch up the caulking after shooting rapids where, sometimes, we were not able to avoid contact with rocks. At one point we needed to cross a sizable lake when the windy weather was a significant factor. After holding off a couple of days we waited until the wind died down in the late afternoon before making the dash. In preparation, we caulked up the lashing holes along the gunwales to get an extra couple inches of freeboard in the rough water. The canoe became a part of our system, and we marveled at the efficiency of this craft that had been developed from the experience of the generations of the Algonquin Indians who produced it from their local resources.

In the succeeding 70 years from the time of that trip, many details have been lost, but the memory of a wonderful life-changing experience remains. Ray and I each got married and raised families, and although we lived 700 hundred mile apart we got together—once or more—every year, involving canoe trips and camping with both families. Together we bought an 80-acre piece of bush land in Ontario. After camping on it for a few years we built a primitive, one-room cabin, a quarter mile off the nearest gravel road. When I contemplate the things in life that have given me pleasure, the cabin and the times spent there with the Newells and my family members are high on the list. And that canoe trip seems to be a seminal event on those later activities.

Senses of Humor

My long-term friend, Ray, and I were heading north in late May, enjoying the early spring bird migration. As evening approached, we pulled into a nondescript, two-story motel in the Upper Peninsula of Michigan. I told the grumpy-looking woman at the desk that we would like a room with two beds.

In an angry tone she asserted "Well, we don't have any rooms available on the first floor!" Somewhat taken aback I said, "Well then, how about a room on the fourth floor?"—knowing full well that it was a two-story building. The reply, in an even more aggrieved, louder voice: "We don't *have* a fourth floor!!"

Oops, bad comment, not funny, better move on. "So, what do you have?" And we took a room for the night—on the second floor.

The next morning, we left the motel and started to look for a likely place to eat breakfast. A sign advertising the Green Lantern Restaurant showed an arrow pointing to the left. The name of the restaurant didn't fit our image of a place for breakfast, but the sign told us that they served breakfast—so we turned left. We were not reassured that this was our place, but we decided to give it a try. We entered a dark room, with colored lights around a bar—a typical north woods tavern. Obviously *not* what we were looking for, but a sign "Dining Room" pointed down a dark hall. The door at the end opened into a bright sunny room, with windows all round—exactly what we were looking for.

We were greeted by a pleasant woman who told us to sit wherever we wished—not surprising since we were the only customers. We chose a seat next to a window where we looked out on a softball diamond and small-town park. The story that we constructed (out of thin air) to explain this place was that of a young couple who lived in the area, wanting to start their own business. His vision was to have a tap where the locals would gather and socialize; hers was a restaurant, where the local families would gather and socialize—and the compromise was the Green Lantern. (Presumably he chose the name.)

She took our order of eggs, bacon, and pancakes and assured us that we would have only a short wait for the food to be prepared. I said, "No hurry, we'll just sit here and wait for the softball game to start." She smiled. "Fine—that will be on June 15th." Amused, I responded "I'm not sure we can wait that long." "Well," she countered cheerfully, "We have a different menu every day.

We did enjoy the humor—and the breakfast.

Roundup

1948

Here I am—ready to help process 50 cows and 50 calves just delivered to the rancher's holding pen—and this is *not* why I came to New Mexico for a summer job.

I'm living in a house trailer parked in the middle of a large flat ranch area on the Plains of San Augustine, about 50 miles west of Socorro. I came to work on a research project about thunderstorm electricity, and my trailer is adjacent to a sizable area where we have established a network of instruments with which we might be able to answer questions about lightning strokes—questions that were raised by Benjamin Franklin and debated ever since.

The site is an excellent place for the measurements we need to make, and we are much obliged to the rancher who is willing to have us use his ranch land for our project. A couple of days ago the person in charge of our project found out that the rancher was expecting the delivery of 100 cattle and was caught without the aid of two ranch hands he had counted on to help with the job of processing them. My boss suggested that two of his boys might volunteer to help him out. The two are me, a graduate student here for a summer job, and Joe, an undergraduate student at the New Mexico Institute of Science and Technology at Socorro. We are total greenhorns when it comes to ranching, but we're willing—and even enthusiastic—to be of help.

There are two operations going on. The cows are being run through a squeeze chute where they can be restrained and treated appropriately. The calves are a different matter. They are huddled around the edges of a fenced enclosure. The head rancher, riding his horse, cuts one out from the group and expertly rolls out a lasso loop under the running calf, which usually catches one or both rear legs in the loop. This is where the grunts, Joe and I, come in. After a brief instruction we start the calf wrestling. The object of the game is to get the calf on the ground and immobilize him for the duration of the treatment. We find out quickly that if we grab the two near legs, we can't pull or push the calf over; we need to grab the far legs and pull on them while leaning on the calf. Once the calf is on the ground our job is to immobilize him by sitting on part of the anatomy and controlling the rear legs by appropriate placement of hands and feet. We are warned to be aware that the calf's leg is like a cocked piston that can strike out with great force. On his first or second calf, Joe missed this warning and was laid out on the ground by a kick to the head—which took him out of the game. Sooo, one down and 47 calves to go—and it's up to me.

While I hold the struggling calf down, others castrate it (if he is male), brand it with an iron heated in the nearby fire, force a pill down its throat, and vaccinate it for pinkeye and black leg. After surviving these indignities, the released calf goes bawling off to its nearby mother, and it's time for the next.

There are two or three calves that are almost yearlings, and it is just about even odds whether I can take them down—or not. Finally, the last one of them is done, and I'm about done too— after rolling about in the dirt and manure with every bit of my body sore from uncounted impacts with the animals and the ground.

We finish and everybody is ready to hang it up. I'm told that because of the circumstances we missed the usual serving of the treat of "mountain oysters" cooked right there in the branding fire, while we were working. I am thanked for my help on this day. I get in my car and drive to the nearby town, Magdalena, and gladly pay the local hotel two dollars for a long soak in a big bathtub filled—and refilled—with hot water. I have never enjoyed a bath more or been so exhausted in my entire life. But something about the events of this day make me feel very good.

A Walk Around the World

December 1998

Here I am—at the end of the earth—the south end to be more exact. I have come to the US Research Station located at the South Pole in Antarctica. I am here to study beautiful displays in the sky that are produced by the interaction of sunlight with minute ice crystals floating in the clear, cold sky. I hope to photograph both the displays and the microscopic ice crystals that produce them.*

Even getting here was an adventure. The straightforward part of the journey ended at Christchurch on the south island of New Zealand. This is the staging area for all of the US involvement in Antarctica. On this trip we were trying to get to the Pole at the very beginning of the season. It took four tries to make the jump from Christchurch to McMurdo, the large US station located on the coast in Antarctica. Two of those tries involved the discouraging experience of flying for ten hours in the noisy, dark, uncomfortable hold of a cargo plane, before landing— back in Christchurch—after wind and blowing snow made landing at McMurdo impossible. Similar problems prompted delays in making the last 800-mile jump from McMurdo to the Pole Station. We took off on wheels from the sea ice at McMurdo, but landed on skis on the icy plateau at the Pole. So, finally, here I am.

I watch as a Hercules LC130 cargo plane arrives at the Pole. The pilots never turn off the engines. The pilot and the navigator jump off the plane to take pictures of themselves, standing in front of the reflecting sphere partly surrounded by a semicircle of flags of the nations that signed the original Antarctic treaty. The information sign proclaims "GEOGRAPHICAL SOUTH POLE". It is apparently their first trip. The cargo is quickly unloaded, new cargo loaded, and the plane roars off. Some of us who have been there for a while may smile to think that they never made it to the *real South Pole*, which is marked by a copper stake driven in the ice some 100 yards away. It was placed there by people from the US Geological Service who carefully located and marked the spot where the rotation axis of our earth intersects the flat icy plane of the polar surface in central Antarctica. Next to the stake is mounted a bronze marker identifying the significance of the stake and announces "AMUNDSEN-SCOTT SOUTH POLE STATION". Nearby is a tall pole with many signs pointing in various directions telling the direction and distance to Walla Walla, or Minneapolis, or, presumably, the hometowns of people who have found their way to this unique spot on the planet.

I can see another similar marker showing the location of the Pole, as determined a year ago, and a sequence of markers identifying the location of the Pole on each of the past several New-Years Days. Apparently the location of the South Pole is changing—moving about 30 feet each year across the icy surface. How can that be? Actually the big effect is not that the earth's rotation axis is changing but that the mass of surface ice covering the polar plateau is moving.

The elevation at the Pole is about 10,000 feet above sea level, and ice can slowly flow under pressure. It flows slowly outward and speeds up when it is channeled between mountain peaks at the edge of the plateau—becoming glaciers. As it reaches the sea it floats on the water and is called the Antarctic Ice Shelf. And when chunks of it break away from the gigantic Antarctic ice mass, it becomes icebergs. The Pole is not the center of this spreading flow but, as the markers indicate, the surface ice at the Pole is moving about 30 feet per year.

When I stand right at the Pole, every direction I look is north. Suppose I take a few steps along a north/south line (a meridian) that passes through Greenwich, England. That line is called the prime meridian and is arbitrarily defined as having a longitude of zero degrees. Suppose I set my watch to read 12:00 noon when the sun is highest in the sky. If I turn left and walk the few steps to get me to the meridian line that is 15 degrees west of the prime meridian, I have to reset my watch one hour earlier, if I want local time to be noon when the sun is highest in the sky. So every time I move 15 degrees (one time zone) west I have to set my watch one hour earlier. As I move, my watch is set to 11am, 10 am…2am, 1am, midnight, and then 11 pm—*but it would be 11 o'clock the previous day!* So to solve this paradox I have to add a day to my calendar date sometime as I travel west around the world. The convention is that the latitude of 180 degrees—halfway around the world—is the International Date Line. When travelers cross this line traveling west they add a day to their local calendar. Shortly after my first visit to the pole, I found it easy to walk around the world.

This visit to the Pole, my third trip over the past 21 years, is extending over the time of New Year's Day. I got to thinking that the people on the U.S east coast enter the new year earlier than the people in the Midwest, and people in Europe earlier than the U.S. etc. The very first person to experience the New Year would be someone standing astride the International Date Line. The date line runs through the Pacific Ocean, avoiding places where people live; however it comes down to the geographic South Pole—right here. By positioning myself in the right place near the pole at the right time, I could be the first person in the entire world to enter the year 1999. A couple of minutes before the calculated time I went to the Pole and starting walking rapidly around the pole, circling it until a few minutes after the zero time. I go back to bed thinking, rather smugly, that I am THE FIRST!

While thinking about it the next day, I realized that in calculating the time for the New Year to start on the International Date Line, I had made a mistake and was an hour off! Oh well, never mind!

For a demonstration of a wide variety of sky effects and more of a discussion of the Pole Station, see the one-hour video program (Sunlight and Ice Crystals in the Skies of Antarctica) streamed online at "UWM Science Bag physics."

Japanese Writing

I was in the city of Kyoto, attending an international conference at Kyoto University. After the second day's meetings, a colleague from Cornell University and I decided to leave the touristy part of the city and eat dinner at a small, authentic Japanese restaurant. We wandered a few blocks away from the main street and found such a place. As was the custom, model dishes of the food were displayed in the window, with the name of each written in Japanese characters.

I knew nothing about Japanese characters and had speculated on how many of the little flourishes in handwritten script are essential to the meaning and how many are just the personal characteristics of the writer. Here was the opportunity to do a little experiment. In my notebook I copied, as well as I could, the name of the dish I decided to order. When the waiter came, I showed him my copy and he bowed, acknowledging the information, and in due time the chosen dish arrived. It was a bit gratifying, although I hadn't really learned much about the question in my mind.

One of the influential organizers of the meeting was a Professor at Kyoto University. In his research he had used a technique that I had pioneered, and he had done some good work with it. He treated me as a special guest and, as a courtesy to me, had assigned one of his students to see that I would receive anything I needed to cope with my surroundings while I was in Kyoto. The young man was quite solicitous in carrying out his assignment. When I talked with him the next day, I told him of our visit to the restaurant and showed him the characters I had copied in my notebook. He complimented me on my writing—saying that it was even *better than that of his Professor*. I protested saying that I was not *writing* but *drawing* the characters. Then, after a moment of hesitation, in a tentative voice, he added an interesting detail, saying "…but you were not in a Japanese restaurant—it was Chinese."

A Satisfying Ovation

We are in a large lecture room for a course named Light and Color. Some of the students come with an interest in the subject, but some are here to fulfill a distribution requirement and are fearful they will not be able to understand any science subject. My challenge is to show them that they can understand—and even enjoy—some things they have never considered before.

Today we are talking about the electromagnetic spectrum, which consists of waves of many different wavelengths. Those most familiar to us are in the visual spectrum that consists of all the colors of the rainbow. The short wavelength rays are the violet and progressive longer waves are blue, green, yellow, orange, and red. But there are waves that are shorter than the violet—called ultraviolet—and waves longer than the red—called infrared—that are invisible to us. In fact, the same spectrum includes x-rays, and radio waves ranging from the very, very short to the very, very long wavelengths. Question: Don't you find it interesting that our eyes can only experience a narrow section of this vast spectrum?

Other animals are sensitive to different ranges of wavelengths. For example, whitetail deer are not sensitive to the red end of the spectrum, which, of course, explains why hunters can wear red, or blaze orange, clothing without alerting the deer. And honeybees can see in the ultraviolet—and are attracted to flowers that flamboyantly advertise their presence with bright ultraviolet displays. A hand pops up in the fourth row.

"But what color would they see—in the ultraviolet?" It is a spontaneous and natural question from someone who is paying attention. And I have an answer: "I guess you would have to call it a *pigment of your imagination.*" After a brief pause, the room erupts into a chorus of hisses, and boos, and a stamping of feet—all dissolving into laughter. Obviously others are also paying attention.

It was, perhaps, one of the most satisfying ovations I have ever received!

Monarch Butterflies

My first job after graduate school was in an industrial Laboratory in Milwaukee, Wisconsin. My laboratory was a well-lit air-conditioned room. The window next to my desk looked out on a landscape of an old industrial plant, with its rusty storage bins, grimy buildings, and dirt-filled corners. On one of the first sunny, cool days of an autumn season a movement just outside my window caught my attention and I glanced up just in time to see a monarch butterfly flit past. After it happened again, I went to look out the window and saw another—and another—go by.

These beautiful butterflies seemed out of place in this industrial environment, but as I watched I saw that there was a steady procession moving south along the building. Their flight corridor seemed to extend only about fifty feet on the leeward side of my block-long, five-story building. I talked by phone to a person whose window was eighty feet from mine and started a timer when he reported a passing butterfly. As the orange and black creature came dancing past my window, I stopped the timer and computed the flying speed. They were traveling about seven miles per hour. I measured the flux of butterflies flowing past, outside my window. Each hour I did a three-minute count and recorded the number of butterflies that passed my window in the three-minute interval. The numbers increased as the morning proceeded, then dropped off in the afternoon. I recorded something like 30, 60, 12, 9 butterflies in my three-minute samples—butterflies moving faster than a person could walk, along my building to the south.

The monarchs were moving, and I was excited to realize that this stretch of wind-protected flight I was watching was only one city block of a flight that would continue over a thousand miles. It was a journey almost unimaginable for something with the perceived frivolous nature of a butterfly but which, nevertheless, would be accomplished despite gusty winds, cold driving rain, and a scorching hot sun. If I could believe that such an impossible trip could be made, then I could also accept that these same individuals would start the trip back north in the spring and that in the summer I would see their descendants come to lay their eggs in the fields around my old farmhouse.

What did my three-minute counts, 30, 60, 12, 9, mean? I could see that at noon there was a peak flow of 20 butterflies each minute, travelling down this narrow flyway. The number dropped over the next four hours to one per minute, then to none. But what is one butterfly a minute or even twenty? Had I seen a few butterflies? or several? or even many? Here is where some simple mathematics shaped my perception. When I plotted the butterfly counts against the time of day, a smooth curve resulted. The area under that curve yielded the total number of butterflies whose passage I had sampled. I could see that what I had witnessed on this day was three thousand butterflies pulsing past my dingy window. Where I watched them fly a few yards of their thousand-mile journey—where I watched them and marveled.

Part Four:

Reflections Later in Life

A Path Not Taken

On my shelf I find field guides to a variety of subjects. The collection includes birds, trees, butterflies, mushrooms, mammals, flowering plants, trees, amphibians, snakes, insects, spiders, grasses, mosses, ferns, fossils, and animal tracks. Being interested in these things led me to an interest in photographing them.

During my college years I didn't have much discretionary spending money. However, in my senior year I did buy a used, 35 mm, German camera with a good lens. The feature that made it affordable to me was that it did not take American film cassettes. I had to reload the film from a Kodak cassette into the German cassette and then, after exposure, load it back to the Kodak cassette for processing. Later, in graduate school when I had access to a machine shop, I milled out the interior of the camera so that it would take a Kodak cassette and I figured out a way to advance the film appropriately.

There was no way to take closeup pictures with this camera, but I rigged some lenses that would allow the camera to focus on things two or three feet from the camera. To get the system to work I had to accurately measure the distance from the camera to the mushroom, or snail, or flower...or another object that was not moving. My (perhaps biased) opinion was that I had the start of a collection of rather good wildflower photos. The next step was to acquire a new single-lens reflex camera that enabled me to see the picture I was about to take—and the process became much, much easier.

Shortly after acquiring that camera, I was about to make a move from the research labs at Allis Chalmers to the Physics Department at the University of Wisconsin-Milwaukee. I had thought that there was a niche for a good field guide to flowering plants of Wisconsin, and this move could give me the possibility to be part of producing such a book. I spent some serious time estimating how long it would take to produce the necessary photographs for such a project and concluded that it could be done in three summer seasons.

For the book to be successful, I needed to partner with a competent botanist. I approached a well-known botany professor whom I thought would do a good job with the text. I knew that he had a reputation of being a difficult person to work with, but I decided to talk to him. I proposed that we be joint authors of a book on "Wildflowers of Wisconsin"; I would be responsible for the photos, he would be responsible for the text. He showed some interest in the project but said that, of course, he could provide some of the photos. I agreed that was a possibility, but I would be the one to make the decision. He didn't like that arrangement, and I was unwilling to end up with it being his book, with an acknowledgment that I had contributed to the photographs. So that book didn't happen.

Instead, I went to this newly created University of Wisconsin-Milwaukee. It was the second campus of the University of Wisconsin. How it would be developed was largely undefined. I became very much involved in developing an interdisciplinary research program involving people from physics, chemistry, and engineering departments. It attracted competent researchers who were committed to the concept of such a group. They were people who, otherwise, would not have come to this campus.

The program received early support from the National Science Foundation. It grew and prospered—and influenced the future of this new institution.

One of the problems the research group faced was losing active members who took other positions. The positions were not at other universities but at UW-Milwaukee. According to my count, the Laboratory for Surface Studies provided, at different times, eight department heads, four Associate Deans in the College of Letters and Science, three Deans of the Graduate School, and two Vice Chancellors.

If I had taken those first three summers to develop a book on wildflowers of Wisconsin, that particular research program would not have been developed, and the rest of my scientific career would be much different from what it has become. What would it have been? I really don't know; it was a path not taken.

A Life Between

A recent note published on a CNN website proclaims: "Some trees can live for more than 1,000 years, and scientists think they figured out why. *They Drink Water. They don't stress. They mind their own business.* Be like a tree, folks, and live forever."

This note is based on research concerning the ginko tree in China, and the results are not well represented by the anthropomorphic summary quoted here. The writer of that brief comment could have found a comparison of a tree species in the mountains of California that makes the oldest ginkgo trees look like youngsters. The bristlecone pine trees live to be nearly 5,000 year old. That is as close to a tree living forever that has ever been found.

These trees live near the tree line, enduring high winds and extreme cold. Not many other plants can survive in the hard rock areas inhabited by the bristlecones; the oldest specimens live in the most exposed and precarious places. As these trees age, much of their bark may die, leaving a narrow strip of living tissue connecting the roots to a handful of live branches.

So, there is a description of a long life suggested to me by that recent note: a very long life to be sure, but one beset by deprivation, hardship, and suffering.

A description of a drastically different life is described in a short poem by Edna St. Vincent Millay:

My candle burns at both ends;
It will not last the night;
But ah, my foes, and oh, my friends—
It gives a lovely light!

My choice is for a life somewhere in between.

There Has to Be A Better Way

Mother

Mother had a good 90th birthday celebration. Shortly after, her vigor declined and it seemed that her will to live diminished. She was clear that she wanted no extreme methods used to keep herself alive; she had lived a full life and was ready to move on. She was in an independent-living apartment in a retirement complex, near the home of my older sister. My daughter was staying with mother for a couple of days and was taking a nap on the living room sofa when several things happened at the same time. Mother got up from a nap, apparently lost her balance, and fell. As Karen heard the fall and jerked awake, someone was knocking on the door. At the door were two representatives of the "medical establishment." One of them, the nurse, immediately took charge and proceeded to call for an ambulance. Karen's protest—that this was not what my mother wanted—was met with the proclamation that not getting this woman the medical care she needed constituted criminal negligence and she was going to be taken to the hospital. The nurse clearly decided that this girl (who had just been awakened to the chaotic scene) was no fit person to make such an important decision. Karen was able to contact my sister, who arrived before mother was loaded into the ambulance. Dorothy showed that she had the power of attorney to make such a decision and made it clear that mother was not going to be taken to the hospital. With all of our planning, we had narrowly escaped her being taken over by the medical establishment. They may have been able to extend her life by several days, or even weeks, but with measures that my mother clearly did not want. She died peacefully in her sleep a few days later—but it was a near thing.

Ralph

I became friends with Ralph after we moved to Oakwood Village. As Ralph aged, he had more and more difficulty getting around. He was moved to Assisted Living and after a while, he was in bed whenever I visited. A daughter and her husband, living in Minneapolis, came often to visit and spend time with him. I didn't know the details of his medical condition, but, although he did not appear to be in significant distress, it was assumed that he would not be leaving his bed. The son-in-law retired early so they could spend most of their time in Madison. Ralph's family changed their lives to support him. They were there, supporting him, as he went from living, to only existing, and finally—after more than a year—to life's final end. The release was said to be a blessing when it finally came. It seemed to me that, for everyone involved, there could have been a better way.

Bill

Before I knew him, Bill had been a physician. He was long retired but had many interests in the world around him. When he could no longer ride a bike, he got a recumbent trike, but after a while that didn't work either. Although his mind was still active, his body was wearing out. Some years later, with failed hearing, diminishing sight, and less and less mobility, his life held a dwindling number of rewards. He confided to a friend, by email, that he had ordered a hunting knife online.

Some days later he used it in his bathroom. Some might say that fortunately, as a physician, he knew exactly where to direct the blade. It was difficult for his wife and family to take much solace in that insight. There should have been a better way.

Bruce

Bruce was my brother-in-law, and also my good friend. When he was diagnosed with an aggressive cancer, his horizon was suddenly reduced to "no more than six months". Soon a hospital bed was brought to the apartment—and a wheel chair—and a motorized recliner, which could be adjusted to make lack of mobility a little more tolerable. His wife (my sister) devoted herself to his care, and the constant demands of his situation were taxing her physical resources. Phyllis was determined to keep him at home as long as possible and was arranging for more outside help.

Nancy and I had married three years after Barbara's death. At that time we calculated that we had been friends for 19 years, and she had moved quickly into the family circle. When we went to stay for a few days, Nancy took my sister out for a few hours of relief, away from the apartment, while I stayed with Bruce. I welcomed this opportunity to be alone with him, for one last time. His mind seemed clear, but he could only speak slowly, with great effort. I asked him what he wanted to do before he died. The answer came slowly, but clearly: "I just want it over." It was over in another three weeks, less than two months after he had learned of this inevitable ending. At his funeral I heard the opinion that it was a blessing that the end of his suffering came so quickly. There *has* to be a better way.

A Wealthy Man

I had never considered myself a wealthy man. I was born on October 24, 1929. A third of a lifetime later, when my children were quite young, one of them came across the fact that on that exact day the US stock market crashed, triggering the great depression that impacted our lives for the next decade. They had a lot of fun—at my expense, of course—that my birth was the cause of it all.

My father was a small-town schoolteacher and had the good fortune to have a job over those depression years. It was not high paying—but it was a job, and we lived frugally. I remember that I had a brown zippered sweater that was beginning to have darning over the earlier darnings. I thought nothing about it, but once my mother commented that there was no shame in wearing older clothes as long as they were neatly mended and kept clean.

My father was continually employed, and my mother was skillful as a gardener; sewer of clothes; and canner of fruits, vegetables, and meats. We lived comfortable middle-class lives.

Skip forward to the time when my long-time friend Ray and I set out to explore the possibility of buying a piece of undeveloped woodland in Ontario at what were reported to be amazingly low prices. Ray, with his family, lived in Rochester, NY and we lived in Milwaukee. There was a region along the north shore of Lake Huron that was less than 500 miles from each of our homes. Over the next couple of years, we pursued several lines of inquiry. We got lists of land being auctioned for nonpayment of back taxes, talked to town clerks who knew the local people and might know who wanted to sell a piece of property, and talked to real estate dealers in the small towns. Any one of these approaches might well have produced a hit for us over a couple of years—and one of them did. In the small town of Thessalon, located on the shore of Lake Huron, we walked into the office of a realtor and told him what we were looking for. He scratched his ear thoughtfully, fumbled under his counter and came up with a deed which he plopped on the counter, and said that recently a fellow came into his office and said that he wanted to sell an eighty-acre piece of property nearby. The man lived in Michigan and found that he didn't use the land for hunting anymore. The realtor had taken a quick look at the land and knew approximately where its borders were. Following his instructions, we took a look and found a wooded property with mature trees, punctuated by islands of rock—the outcroppings of the Canadian Shield rock which were sculpted by the last glacier. To us it looked wonderful. We returned to the office and asked the price. The realtor said $750. My heart leaped at that low price and I was totally amazed when Ray said "How about $700?" The relator said "Okay." It was years later when I thought to ask Ray why he made that counteroffer at such an amazing price. He said that he read the hand-written note (upside down of course) on the cover of the deed saying the owner would take $700 for it.

For the next two or three years we continued to meet and camp on our new property. We started talking about having a standup, lean-to, screened structure to make things easier when we were dealing with mosquitos or rain. Then we considered a "permanent" wooden, lean-to structure, or maybe even a cabin.

We decided on the cabin. We carried in all the materials along a walking path, a quarter mile from the nearest gravel road. The opening of the trail, invisible from the road, gave us privacy and an effective shield from unwanted visitors when we were not there.

The cabin was primitive—we would never call it a cottage—but it contained everything we needed to live comfortably on the edge of one of the largest outcroppings near the center of the property. As we developed names for the rocks, this one became Rock Centrum.

The cabin came to be the favorite meeting place for the Greenlers and Newells and our children. There were games, and boomerang throwing, and slingshot contests, and kite flying… Ray and I always had observations of animals, plants, rocks, atmospheric effects, and night skies that led to experiments and more observations. In a book I published in 2000, many of these activities were described in a chapter titled Just Playing, and several of them resulted in papers published in scientific journals, public talks, and programs based on the theme of "seeing with the mind as well as the eye." The cabin also hosted gatherings of our separate families and special friends whom we thought would appreciate this special place with its primitive accommodations. It was a source of great pleasure for many years and remains so today.

At one point I mused about what the property was "worth" to me—in financial terms. It was easy to dismiss the question with the answer "Priceless", but I thought, realistically, there must be *some figure* that would compel us to sell. For example, if someone offered a hundred million dollars…?

We bought the property for $700. Let me consider values increasing by factors of ten. How about $7,000? Of course, we had constructed the cabin, which, though primitive, did increase the value and local land prices were increasing rapidly. $7,000? Ridiculous! Next step, $70,000. Similar vacant land at the time would have cost half of that, without a cabin— and without the intimate familiarity of the animal-vegetable-mineral community that comes from hours of exploration in all seasons. No deal!

How about $700,000? That's the better part of a million dollars! Somewhere in that last price range is the place where I'd not be able to rationalize the "value" of keeping this piece of land in my possession.

Of course, no one has offered such a price and we have turned the land over to the next generation. But consider the implications of this line of thought. The fact that I could even think of that little piece of land in such terms must have made me a wealthy man.

Sycamore Tree

There is a sycamore tree growing on the Oakwood Village campus in Madison, where I live, and it is one of my favorites, even though it is a little out of place. You probably won't find a sycamore when you drive in the countryside around Madison. You won't have to go very far south to find them because Madison is just at the northern edge of the sycamore's range. I assume that this tree has prospered here because of the heat-island effect that keeps a city warmer than the open country. Additional protection is provided by the buildings, close by on either side. Sycamores have touched my life at a number of different times and different places.

When I was in high school, we lived in a house with a sycamore tree in the front yard. My mother called it a "dirty tree". To her, it seemed always to be littering the lawn with one thing or another. If it wasn't the large plates of bark that it shed, it was the inch-diameter seed balls that it dropped, or the large, tough leaves that looked like overgrown maple leaves and seemed to accumulate on the ground—worse than most other trees.

She, of course, was right about the bark. The bark of all trees has to yield to a growing trunk by some method. For some it is stretching; for many it is the bark splitting along vertical lines as new bark infills the split. The sycamore bark lacks the elasticity, so its solution to the growth problem is to slough off hand-size flakes of old bark, which leave the surface mottled with greenish-white and gray patches. That feature alone makes it easy to identify a sycamore—up close.

The tree next to the four-story building in which I now live is nearly three feet in diameter and 80 feet tall. As open-grown sycamores get older they tend to grow large secondary trunks with the main trunk being the fattest of any tree in the eastern US. In his journal, George Washington recorded a sycamore along the proposed route for a new canal in Virginia. He measured the tree to have a circumference, three feet above the ground, of 44 feet 10 inches. That is a *diameter of over 14 feet!*

I planted two sycamore trees in the backyard of the old farmhouse, north of Milwaukee, where we lived for 39 years. After a few years one of them lost some of its branches, apparently the effect of a cold winter. The other, growing 25 feet away, remained undamaged. The process was repeated every few years, with the less hardy tree dying back to a branch or two and the other tree continuing to thrive. I finally put the poor tree out of its misery and the other had grown to be, perhaps, 30 feet tall when we moved away. Those two trees would seem to illustrate the life on Nature's teeter-totter at the very northern edge of the life zone for *Platanus occidentalis.*

Another project that I thought about for a few years, but never committed to try, was a photo collection of trees. I considered how—in one or two photographs at the most—I could capture the essence of a tree species. The idea was suggested by a few examples. Back in the days when American elms graced our city and countryside, one could instantly identify this tree standing in a field almost as far away as one could see it. The graceful form of a fountain of branches—rising from a slender trunk and curving downward at their extremities—is unmistakable. The bur oak that used to form oak savannas in midwestern prairie country has a short heavy trunk with stout side branches that is distinctive even if one cannot get a close-up look at the deeply ridged bark. Most people recognize the curtains of hanging branches of the weeping willow, or the tight columns in a line of Lombardy poplars. My list was longer, but there was one basic problem with the scheme. You can't get a photograph that shows the silhouette of a tree growing in a forest. It was one of those intriguing ideas that didn't work out, and I never attempted such a book.

After grade school, I grew up in Toledo, Ohio. That city has a rather remarkable art museum, but it was not part of my culture during my high school years. Some years later, while visiting my parents there, I took the opportunity to visit the museum. Many things about it were interesting, but the one that really caught my attention was a painting by Andrew Wyeth. I liked Wyeth's paintings and had thumbed through some books of his paintings—but here was one I did not remember seeing before. As I studied it, I felt a kinship with that man whom I had never met. He had pondered a problem that I had thought about but never solved: "How do you capture the essence of a sycamore tree?" Here was his solution: You reproduce the view as seen by a squirrel sitting high up in the tree. The big branches in the foreground display the distinctive bark in beautiful detail. Equally clear are the stout, maple-like leaves, brown in the fall season and a seed ball, still hanging on. The painting has a high horizon—the squirrel is looking toward the ground, through the open canopy of the branches, likely focused on the man far below, carrying a gun. The name of the painting is *The Hunter*. The squirrel may be focused on the hunter, but I think the viewer's focus must be the wonderful surrounding sycamore tree, seen from the inside.

Andrew figured it out.

Small Towns

When I look at a map of Northwestern Ohio, I can find the small town where I grew up in the 1930s. A circle of 10-mile radius, centered on West Unity, includes 8 small towns, mostly with populations of less than 3,000 residents. It is typical of that part of the upper Midwest. Why so many towns? Wouldn't it be more efficient to have fewer, larger towns? I suspect that the answer is connected to the distance a horse, pulling a wagon, would travel in an hour or so.

This part of the country was largely agricultural when I grew up. I lived in the town, but most of the kids in my class were farm kids. The town really lit up on a Saturday night. It was the time when the farm families came to town to do their weekly shopping. There were special programs and band concerts. Various businesses had specials—designed to attract customers from the surrounding countryside. I remember when many of the local stores sponsored a drawing of cash prizes. When a person bought merchandise from any one of these stores, they got a ticket for every dollar spent. My dad had traded in our old car for a new Plymouth so that purchase put a good many tickets into the pot, signed by different members of our family. That added excitement, because over the summer we won something in several drawings.

The drawing took place on the town bandstand. The wire cage holding the tickets was rotated by some kid from the crowd to prove that the tickets were thoroughly mixed. I'm a bit vague on the number of tickets that were drawn. There were some $10 prizes, more for $5, and even more for $1. If a kid my age got a

$1 prize it was a Big Deal; that would buy a whole bunch of candy bars.

Of course, the merchants of West Unity were competing with those of Pioneer, or Montpelier, or Stryker for the business of the surrounding farming communities. Not many years earlier, most of the farm folk drove the family to town with a horse and wagon. Such a trip might take as long as an hour if the farm was 5 miles away. A round trip taking two hours was pushing the limits of the amount of time a farmer was willing to invest in a weekly trip to town. If the nearest town was as far as 10 miles away, there was the niche for a new source of goods in between—another small town.

According to my speculation, the speed of the family horse determined the spacing of towns in that area, in those horse-and-buggy days. The small towns included a grocery store, a dry-goods store where one could buy clothing, the hardware store, the drug store, a couple of churches, the funeral parlor, the creamery, the town park with the bandstand, the schoolhouse, post office, perhaps a hotel, a bar or two, offices for the doctor and the lawyer…all of the things required in everyday life. As cars replaced the horses, the small towns added a gas station and still provided a community that was attractive enough to keep the town alive. You might speculate that in the intervening years the smaller towns would disappear, but that seems not to have happened.

What about West Unity? When I was a kid there, the population was about 1,000 people. In the intervening 80 years the population has ballooned to nearly 1,800. What do you suppose it will be in another 80 years?

Bike Riding

2020

Actually, it started with a trike—a trike that had no pedals. One of my earliest memories is of a little wooden trike. It was a dull red color, and I could sit on it and move around by pushing with my feet. It would seem likely that later I had a conventional tricycle, but no such trace of memory remains. The first bicycle I had was in the early Depression time when I was in grade school. We acquired an old girl's bicycle that was intended to be shared by me and my two older sisters. As I recall I was the only one who used it and it served me well, getting around the small town where we lived. Of course it was a single-speed bike, but I concluded that it was geared a bit higher than the others kids' bikes. It would go a little further with one rotation of the pedals and gave me an advantage in the spontaneous racing contests that were a part of our everyday play.

When I was in the fourth or fifth grade, my friend, Bob, had an uncle whose farm was in the country, outside the town where we both lived. Bob's uncle took a rare vacation where he and his family were gone for a week, and Bob agreed to take care of the animals while they were gone. I agreed to go with him. We would set out on our bikes in the morning, do the morning chores, eat lunch, do some farm work followed by afternoon chores, and then jump on our bikes for the long pedal home. It was the longest bike ride I had ever made. My father knew where the farm was and reckoned that it was four miles away.

That impressed me—that we had biked 8 miles in a single day.

After we moved to the big city of Toledo, I became the proud owner of a relatively new bike—one that was in style of the 1940s. It had big balloon tires and a sizable enclosure under the front bar to contain a horn and a headlight. It was clearly a luxury vehicle.

After high school I didn't ride any bike for 15 years. I had a friend who rode a modern multi-speed bike, and I went for a ride with her on her son's bike. That was so much fun that I bought one of my own, and she and I helped coalesce a group of friends which, for years later, we called the Bike Bunch. We biked together, hiked together, skied together, often ate together, and shared many happy times over the next few decades. Somewhere along the line I developed arm and shoulder problems that were aggravated by riding a touring bike with some of my body weight supported by my arms. The solution was to go to a two-wheeled, recumbent bike where I could sit, leaning back in a comfortable web chair, with my arms forward, hands resting on the handlebars. I described the change as being like sitting in a lawn chair rather than astride a fence rail.

Adapting to the recumbent bike involved a significant learning curve. By necessity the design involves a significantly longer wheelbase than the conventional bike. To get moving from a standing start was difficult, especially on an up-sloping path. But it did solve the problem of arm and shoulder aggravation. Over the next months, while riding the recumbent, I pondered the problem of keeping my balance when moving slowly. I finally realized that with the long configuration a person has to ride faster to keep from falling over. Another way of describing it: You have to make bigger corrections—implying more wandering from side to side—when trying to ride slowly. As my reaction-time declined with advancing age, the wandering became greater and was becoming a problem—especially when riding on a narrow bike path. Time for the next evolutionary step: the recumbent trike.

With three wheels, the balance problem disappears. One can go slow—stop—start—hesitate—with no balance problem. It was a new solution to the problem of biking (triking) as I got older. With this innovation, my yearly biking record shows that I went from biking a couple of hundred miles a year to as many as a thousand miles a year. Age takes its toll, and the mileage began to decline until I made yet one more adaptation. I was able to add a battery-powered assist motor. The technology does not mean that you stop pedaling. It is designed with a so-called proportional assist. Essentially, you always pedal, but the motor adds a fraction of your effort to help propel the bike. There are several settings with different levels of assistance. For example, the motor can add 50% to the energy you provide from your pedaling. Or it could provide 100% assist—the motor adding as much energy as you are providing. It can even provide more energy than you are providing—like 200% or 300%.

When I first added the motor assist, some of my friends suggested that now I didn't get any exercise from biking, but that is not the case. Usually when I, and Nancy (whose trike is similarly outfitted), return from a trip, we are as tired as we used to be without the assist, but we have been able to climb hills, and have gone farther, and have seen more interesting things than we could have done before.

So, in the year when I turned 90, I looked at my list of Biking Miles (of course, I keep a list—and I know it should now be called Triking Miles) and decided to set the goal: "Ride 900 miles at age 90". So, nearly nine decades later, I have come full circle: Starting with a trike with no pedals, I end up with a trike with pedals (plus a helping boost from modern technology). And I just managed to do the 900 at 90.

If I Were 20 Years Younger

2010

There are always many things I would like to do, but if I am realistic, I know that many of them would never really get to the top of the list. However, there is something that might well get there—if I were twenty years younger.

In October, I frequently ride my bike through some nearby, mature prairies. This is a time when the prairies are shutting down, with the summer flowers gone *except* for an occasional patch of purple coneflowers, or black-eyed susans, or New England asters—still in full, beautiful bloom when most of their species-mates have disappeared from the scene.

Why are these few plants still blooming? Two possibilities come to mind.

1. Some very local, non-obvious condition: soil, wind circulation producing a very local microclimate… or
2. A genetic quirk for this clone of plants.

Wouldn't it be neat to be able to have, in your restored prairie, a group of plants that would extend the flowering season by a month? It would increase people's interest in prairies in general if you could have a display when most plants, either natives or cultivars, have given up for the season. And wouldn't you think that people who raise and sell prairie plants and seeds would add such a line to their listings? I would think so.

So what would I do? I would look for as many late-blooming patches as I could find and

1. I would put bags over blossoms in different patches in an attempt make them self-pollinate.*
2. I would try to pollinate blossoms from plants in one patch with pollen from blossoms of another patch, as distant as possible from the first.
3. I would collect seeds from plants in several patches

The collection of seeds from these three groups, all from local sources, might represent a genetic diversity greater than the seeds taken from one patch. I would plant them in my garden plot and, in the two or three years when they start to blossom, would look eagerly to see if any in the batch bloomed later than others of the same species in the general population.

This is the kind of experiment that I like! In one plant generation, I would be able to tell whether it was some local effect or some genetic effect that produced this late-season treat. If there were no difference in blooming time in my test plantings compared to the larger local population, the experiment would be over and I would move on to something else. However, if they did show some late-blooming tendency then I would conclude it is some genetic effect and the real work would begin. For the next generation, I would cross-pollinate some of the test plants that came from different locations and self-pollinate others to see if either one enhanced the late-blooming tendency. Experience would dictate where to go from there to develop a late-blooming subspecies.

But I won't be 20 years younger. I wonder if someone else

might be prompted to consider the possibilities.

Someone interested in such a project would be interested in information about prairie plants that can self-pollinate and those that cannot. See, for example: *Breeding Systems of Plants Used for Prairie Restorations: A Review* by Brenda Molano-Flores in *Transactions of the Illinois State Academy of Science (2004) Volume 97, #2, 95-102*

A Lifetime of Reading

2021

This *lifetime* has lasted a *longtime*. In the first few years I remember my mother reading to me and my two older sisters. Then, a generation later, I remember reading to our three children. It started with books that were primarily picture books but moved on with stories and pictures. If I were to give any advice to new parents on the nurturing of small children, it would be "Read to them". There is a physical intimacy in having a child on your lap and another snuggled up on either side, with all sharing the same focus.

In college there was, of course, much required reading, and I don't remember much about recreational reading. I did become aware of a new book by a writer named Aldo Leopold. I bought a copy of the Sand County Almanac—and it changed my life.

As I became involved in research as a graduate student in physics, I spent more and more time reading the scientific literature in my area of research and other areas that interested me. In that pre-computer age, I devised a system to keep track of publications of interest. One could buy cards, about the size of an envelope, with holes lining all four edges of the card. They were called Keysort cards. I would write a note on a card about the content of the article and the journal reference. Different holes could reference different areas of interest. By cutting out the space between the hole and the edge of the card I could sort the cards for that area of interest. The sorting was done with a long needle—something like a knitting needle. If I stuck the needle through that hole in a deck of cards, all of the cards with that hole cut would drop off the needle. For example, if one of the holes was labeled *Sky Phenomena*, and I thrust my needle through that set of holes in the pack, all of the cards concerning sky phenomena would drop to my desk. I could pick up those cards and sort them again to identify some sub-category, putting the needle through a different hole, for instance labeled *Ice Crystals*. Now the stack on my desk included only the sky effect that resulted from ice crystals in the sky. With additional thrusts I could narrow down the list to find the papers I wanted to reference again.

Every week, I would spend time in the library with my cards, scanning six or eight scientific journals for articles of interest. The reading took a lot of time and effort but is a necessary part of keeping abreast of developments in one's research area. Of course, things are different today. With computers, searching and accessing published articles is much easier, but the most important part has not changed. You still have to read and absorb the information.

What about recreational reading—or reading to broaden one's horizons? I had a compulsion that got in the way of my informal reading. Once I started reading a book, I felt compelled to finish it. Somehow, I felt some obligation to the author to read to the end. When I was busy with family and profession, and finally sat down on a Friday evening and thought of reading…If the only choice was a difficult book that I had started, the alternative seemed to be "not to read". Once I identified the compulsion as a problem, the solution was obvious. Replace that book with something that was a pleasure to read—independent of literary quality or social significance.

It was still difficult to find the time to read. After finishing graduate school, I stepped back to consider the balance in this new stage of my life and decided that if I had any pretense of being an intelligent citizen of the world, I should *make* time in my life for reading. How much? I decided that a minimum goal would be to read at least a book per month. To make that happen I decided to keep track of the books I read and started the Book List in September of 1958. If I looked at the list and was not meeting the goal, I would give reading a higher priority.

The list did provide a couple of unforeseen uses. Every now and then I would try to remember where it was that I had read something. I could look at the list and usually identify the book. I also realized that if I put an X by the author of a book that I particularly enjoyed, I could (and did) come back later to look for other books by the same author.

So, the list has been growing for 63 years. After doing the Reading and the Writing, I can now do some Arithmetic. I can look at the list and see that over the first three years I read an average of one book a month. Over the next three decades that average rose to nearly four per month—about a book per week—and in the past few years, vision problems have reduced the rate somewhat. The list includes favorites that have been reread and those that Nancy and I have read aloud.

The books range from several each by Louis Lamour, Micky Spillane, and Dick Francis, to those by Tracy Kidder, Howard Fast, and Ken Follett, and more recently by Nevada Barr, Barbara Kingsolver, and Michael Perry. That doesn't really scratch the surface: Charles Dickens, John Steinbeck, Tracy Chevalier, and Ray Bradbury are in there with many others. How many? The Arithmetic of The List gives the answer: As of the end of 2021 the number is 1,675—and counting.

Please, no final exam!

It's About Time

In the 1980s

One day—back in those late middle years—I received a note saying that "The Discussion Group" is invited to gather at a friend's home for an evening.

For years that group met every couple of months to discuss some political, social, or ethical problem. There was no organization. Someone would mail out a newspaper or magazine article as introductory reading and give the subject, date, and place for the next gathering. If no one took the initiative, there was no gathering. This was not a subgroup of some organization but an accretion of people who enjoyed the wide-open discussions and became friends based on this contact. Most such informal groups seem to have a finite lifetime, and, after a few years, the called evenings became less regular and then ceased—that is, except for the gathering around Christmas time, when we exchanged white-elephant gifts, played charades, and caught up on each others' lives. And then, after more years, we seemed to get so busy with other things that the annual party also ceased.

So, this note was a call for the dormant group to gather again. The invitation mentioned "those days of discussions when we were young and thought there were answers to all the problems of the world" and went on to ask, "So what have we learned in all of these years of living? We should know more now than we did then." It ended with the assignment "to write out something you have learned and put into practice. Make copies for everyone and bring them along." That was a challenge that called for self-examination; it would seem poor to blow off the request from this group with whom I had shared so much. Where to start?

It seemed that what I have learned is tied up with choices I have made and the consequences that flow from these choices. This is true for all of the different parts of my life: the professional, the social, the intellectual, the recreational, and others, all of which press against each other to fill a finite space.

My professional life included teaching, research, and a number of public service activities. These activities were in constant competition for my time. The time I spent running the "Science Bag" series of programs for public audiences took away time from research, and the inevitable result of spending less time on my research was to be less successful than I could have been in the international community of scientists—which was one of my communities. A significant part of my teaching involved helping students learn how to do research in my lab, or on projects that popped up in conversations and developed into individual student projects. The formal classroom teaching took much time, and there was always the urge to develop better classroom demonstrations and to look up more background information to pique student interest. While some of these activities supported each other, they also competed with each other for time. Also, in this mix of professional activities was the duty to help a department and an institution function effectively.

My family is an important part of my life and has ranked high on the priority list in competition for time. Weekends were generally family oriented. Typically, on Saturday morning, we would do life-maintenance jobs (mowing the lawn, fixing the leaky faucet, putting up the storm windows…) and in the afternoon do something together as a family. And during the week, the spillover from the office (working on tomorrow's classes) was put off until the children were in bed. But where in this mix is there time for recreational reading, or personal writing, or exercise, or participation in the community, or time alone with my spouse?

I've heard the claim that no one on his deathbed has been known to say, "I wish I'd spent more time at the office" and perhaps there is some wisdom in that insight. However, I do believe that there are well-intentioned individuals who, in the later stages of life, have regretted that they didn't accomplish as much as they could have in their careers, or artistic efforts, or efforts to improve the lives of people in need. How can we live our lives to avoid such regrets?

There are people who have "time on their hands", people who seek activities that "help pass the time" or look for ways to "kill time." That is not my problem. For those of us who are fully engaged, our use of time is a zero-sum game; the only way I can spend more time on one part of my life is to spend less on another. Is that really true? Don't we all spend some time on frivolous stuff: watching a dumb TV movie, reading a book that is entertaining, but which has no redeeming merit, or looking at catalogs or web sites with interesting things to sell, even though we have no intent to purchase? What about down time?

I believe that a certain amount of "nonproductive" relaxation or pleasant idleness is, for me, a prerequisite for a healthy, productive life. When I am too busy—for too long—I find an urgency to file my fingernails or do one of the puzzles in the newspaper that I usually ignore, or to repair the seldom-used gadget that has not worked for the last three years. A certain amount of down time seems to be necessary for my life.

It's time to put down on paper my succinct contribution to the upcoming gathering. I come up with:

COMMENTS ABOUT TIME

> *I look at different parts of my life, which include a variety of professional interests and ambitions, a variety of personal interests and ambitions, and a variety of significant relationships with spouse, kids, and friends. There is never enough time to develop all of the different parts of those interests and relationships to what they could be.*

INSIGHT #1. I only get rewards or satisfactions from those parts of my life on which I spend some time.

INSIGHT #2. When I am using all the time there is, "trying harder" doesn't solve anything. My life is an interlocking set of compromises, where expanding the time spent in one area reduces the time spent in another, and the best I can hope for is a set of compromises that brings me some long-term satisfaction in the balance.

INSIGHT #137. Time flies like an arrow. Fruit flies like a banana.

Thoughts of Winter

I'm brushing away the thick layer of leaves on the forest floor of the Nature Preserve, looking for small living plants. Here are a couple of weeds that look vaguely familiar—maybe this one is creeping charlie, and that might be garlic mustard. At another time I might intentionally weed out such plants, but not now. Now I am looking for life to preserve. I will take these things inside and trick them with heat and light into thinking it is spring, and time to start a new season of life and growth

Here are sprouted acorns, which I put in my basket. In most other years the squirrels stash away all the acorns, but the bumper crop this year was more than they could handle and so I collect some for the terrarium. I don't promise these nascent oaks life eternal, just a reprieve from a cold winter season.

When I came out into the Nature Preserve at 3 o'clock this afternoon, the temperature was 32 degrees and falling. The prediction is that it will drop to 12 degrees tonight. I should have done this earlier, but I didn't and now it's almost November. It's cold and my back hurts from stooping and getting up and down. Maybe this is the last year I'll be able to do it—but maybe not. Who knows?

I am aware of the randomness in my selection process. I select this one and pass over that one. I toss a couple of winged maple seeds toward my gathering basket. One of them lands in the basket; the other falls on the ground, but I don't bother to pick it up. Although I am selecting these sprouting acorns to grow and live over the winter, my choice really eliminates them from the possibility of living in the woods and becoming mature trees.

A few trail walkers come by and ask what I am doing. I point to the baskets containing dirt with a bit of greenery and moss showing, and with some hints from me, they realize that I am collecting plants for a terrarium. Some nod in acknowledgment of this strange behavior, but others are caught up in the vision of bringing a preview of spring inside our heated building when winter dominates the world outside. They will probably enjoy watching the terrarium when they see it, inside, after Christmas.

Returning to my apartment, past the settling pond, I see a skim of ice that was not there when I began my gathering, and I find the temperature has dropped to 26 degrees. I go inside, thaw my fingers, stinging from the cold, and push myself to plant the bits and pieces I have collected into their new glass home before I flop down to rest my aching back. Then, after a meal, warmed and rested, I conclude that it has been a good afternoon. Perhaps I'm ready for another winter.